ALSO BY LARRY KILHAM

Non-Fiction
Winter of the Genomes
MegaMinds: Creativity and Invention

Fiction, based on AI
Love Byte
A Viral Affair: Surviving the Pandemic
Saving Juno

GREAT IDEA TO A GREAT COMPANY

MAKING INVENTIONS PAY

Larry Kilham

Second edition
Revised and updated.

Published by
FutureBooks.info
Available for purchase from:
CreateSpace.com
Amazon.com
and other retailers

ISBN: 150861721X
ISBN 13: 9781508617211
Library of Congress Control Number: 2001117001
CreateSpace Independent Publishing Platform
North Charleston, South Carolina

For my father Peter who when he was 80 or so
said he would write his life story when he was old.

For my mother Frances who really wanted to see these stories
in print.

For my wife Betsy who was both patient and counseling
when my enterprises rose and fell
and when this book was written.

CONTENTS

CONTENTS

NOTE TO THE SECOND EDITION

This book has been popular in my home state of New Mexico in part because I am known here. Readers particularly like the parts where I write about our family businesses to illustrate general points. It shows that a tradition of building rewarding businesses based on innovative products can be passed along from generation to generation. The same product development and entrepreneurial lessons apply to corporate environments.

I have decided to update and refresh the original book to produce this second edition. It should be of interest to students, inventors, managers, investors, and government officials.

INTRODUCTION

The company collapsed like a house of cards. My net worth had gone from about a million dollars to the possibility of bankruptcy if the bank took my house. Another high tech dream went into the trash can.

I did not run away to Brazil. I did not apply for unemployment. I said to myself, "I will start over again. I've just been through training school, and now I'm going to do it right." As I write this, my net worth is back up over a million dollars. I went on to start and sell a fun company making environmental monitoring equipment. Although I graduated from a prestigious business school and had great jobs in distinguished companies, much of my learning about building a company was gained in my own various businesses and from shared family business experiences.

Having your own business can be immensely rewarding. Not only could you wind up making more money than you ever imagined, but you could be having fun doing it as well. The new business will test your stamina and perseverance, and it will probably eat up most of your free time and, for a while, your financial resources. A patient and optimistic attitude will lead you through the hard times and will prepare you for dealing with the setbacks as well as help you to exploit the unexpected opportunities as they arise. In the end, you should be wealthy, happy and fulfilled.

My father went through a business collapse at the age of 57, a time when most people are planning their retirement. He sold his previous business for almost nothing and started a new one producing phonograph records of bird songs. The business did not succeed. Then opportunity knocked when he applied his engineering skills to designing what was maybe the first mass-producible bird feeder. He found local shops to fabricate the necessary parts and neighbors to assemble and ship. His bootstrap business became a multimillion-dollar success and the leader in its market.

Both sides of my family have produced many entrepreneurs—the people who organize, manage, and assume the risks of new enterprises—so I have had a lot of experience to draw from. My mother's father had over 100 patents for oil burners. His business became a multimillion-dollar technology licensing operation. His oil burners were used in home furnaces and water heaters, in commercial systems, and had high-volume military applications, including snow melters and tent heaters. Many of my uncles have had their own architecture and engineering firms, and one of my sisters is an artist-entrepreneur on the Maine coast. Her work shows up in shops everywhere as gift cards, place mats, and many other attractive items.

What I have seen in our family of entrepreneurs are the traits and attitudes that engender success. What is it that separated Thomas Edison from the also-rans we never heard of? How do you organize yourself for success so that you have a reasonable chance of inventing the light bulb or at least creating something that will make the basis for a great little business? How do you go from a great idea to a great company?

After finding or developing a product, there is still much work to be done for a business to become a success. In the following chapters I will discuss developing a vision; creating a product; the uses of patents, trademarks and copyrights; how to plan your business and how to create a team; marketing your product, with a special emphasis on the new world of the Web as well as manufacturing and finance. I will illustrate these areas by drawing from the successes and failures of my family's businesses.

Much has already been written about the mechanical aspects of a new enterprise—staffing, business plans, organization charts, structuring deals, and so on—but very little has been written about the psychological environment which can be overwhelming for most entrepreneurs. From my own experiences, I know that the aspiring captain of industry lives in an almost unimaginable pressure cooker. While some people thrive on the pressure, others become despairing and often bitter. I believe that to be a successful entrepreneur you must have a certain psychological profile, with some natural and some developed disciplines that will allow you to turn adversity to advantage.

I am going to explore what I believe to be the attributes of the successful entrepreneur:

- A willingness to do whatever it takes.
- A huge amount of self-esteem.
- Patience and perseverance.
- General business ability.
- Attitude to accept failure and restart as if nothing had happened.
- The keenness to see and snatch unexpected opportunities, even from failures.
- Technical understanding or engineering training with a flair for the creative or experimental.

- Ability to identify and analyze unknowns and to experiment.
- Ability to focus, persist, and see a project through from start to finish.
- Extra attention to family relations.

Today there are more would-be entrepreneurs than there have been in all of civilization (not counting basic enterprises such as shopkeepers and farmers). Our complex society seems to need virtually an infinite variety of goods and services. Consequently, there are countless niches to fill. For example, there would have been little or no interest in my current business of ozone monitoring devices a mere dozen years ago. An explosion of technologies, dating from World War II, has created the ingredients for many new products and services, and for making the small business much more efficient. Also of great Importance, funding for new ventures is much more available than in earlier times.

When you create a company based on your own product that you have developed, you will also have created a statement of your own self-worth. For me this has been a feeling that is hard to match in life and unlike money, it cannot be taken away from you. For this reason, I want to help creative people become successful with their own businesses. If you did not have a vision for yourself already, you would not have picked up this book, so don't stop now. As the famous hockey player, Wayne Gretzky, said, *You miss 100 percent of the shots you never take.*

START WITH A VISION

All great inventors and discoverers have been irresistibly borne onward by faith in the things that could not be seen... To believe and go forward is the key to success and to happiness.
Lilian Whiting, American journalist and author

Virtually all successful business people have been described as visionaries. They could always see a little further over the horizon than anyone else. To develop a great business from a great idea, that is what you need: a great vision. A business vision usually starts with a product insight beyond what other people have.

For example, today we take the photocopier for granted, but when that invention's potential market was being researched in the 1950s, very little future was seen for the machine. At that time copies were more expensive than carbon copies which everyone was using. No major corporation was willing to negotiate the rights to manufacture office machines featuring the carbonless copying process. The Xerox Corporation was formed specifically to commercialize the invention. The rest, as they say, is history.

While your invention may be viewed skeptically, even by experts, if you think you have created something that is really good, don't worry. Experts rarely see the merit of new developments, but their advice and assistance is very valuable to carry the initial product concept to a commercially acceptable product. My advice is: no matter what people say, press ahead.

A great vision should carry you beyond attempting to do the ordinary. It should propel you into accomplishing the extraordinary. If you live for your vision, you will feel that if you don't start your business and succeed with it, your life will not be complete. Your vision should enthuse you that strongly. You will need this level of positive attitude to get through the rough spots and the lonely interludes of business. Your vision needs to be powerful enough to inject positive energy into your employees. You are going to need them with you every step of the way.

Finding Your Vision

Where do you find your vision? Think in terms of something you feel strongly about or have a passion for. It is best if this something uses tools and techniques with which you are already familiar, or better yet, in which you are an expert. Think about developing something that you yourself would be enthusiastic about buying and using. Let's say you love to fly and you are an electronic engineer. Why not improve instrumentation used in aircraft? Test your vision on yourself. Ask yourself if you would prefer to fly a plane using your own designs of instrumentation.

Along the start-up path of your new business you will encounter many nay-sayers, critics, and know-nothings. Your best defense against these people is your self-assurance. Your positive attitude will come from your unshakable vision and your understanding about the details that go into making the product and building a business around it. It will also come from a lack of fear of failure.

Many a hobby enthusiast has asked my opinion of the idea of building a business from a hobby. I caution them against it. Don't let a hobby or interesting pastime become your business vision unless it really is the basis for a significant business. Most hobbies do not lend themselves to significant and lucrative businesses. Also, hobby businesses tend to start in one room of the house and flow to others. The family never likes this, and neither does the Internal Revenue Service. They are very hard on hobbies classified as businesses. Looked at another way, most focused, successful business people would love to have a non-business hobby to get their minds off their business.

Save your hobby for your relaxation because you will not get to enjoy it for long once it becomes your business.

The Creative Part of the Vision

People often ask me: "How do I get an innovative product vision when there are so many people developing products?" Basically, you have to crank up to the fullest your sensory and perceptual awareness. For example:

- Look for a simple but attractive improvement to enhance an existing product type. My father made a small fortune after he redesigned wooden bird feeders by making them into more attractive and functional plastic feeders.
- Think about product design in terms of appearance and simplicity. I built a great business making gas detection

instruments. My designs are low cost and have fewer switches, buttons, and other controls than the existing devices.

- Look for the connectedness of everything. Engineers, scientists, and academics despair when asked to combine many disparate variables. But it is perfectly OK for you to combine mechanical and electrical concepts, cooking, kitchen management, and who knows what else to come up with the world's first really good bagel toaster.
- Do experiments, however crude and imperfect, to improve your insights and understanding so that you can move forward with your product design.
- Don't worry about what other people think or say. Keep observing and visualizing. Visualization can be very powerful because it is a key tool for changing consciousness.

Here is the story of how I stumbled on one of my visions and what happened.

My Road from a Vision to a Company

Step 1 – Perceiving the vision

I was more or less happily plodding along as the partial owner and general manager of a plastics machinery company in New Jersey. I felt that I should develop a new product for quality control during plastics production. It was a gnawing feeling. I believed that there had to be a way to see the impurities in plastics, called gels. Gels look like "fish eyes" in tapioca, and to some small extent they are in all plastic products. They can cause a great deal of frustration by the damage they can cause, ranging from pinhole leaks in milk jugs to runs in stockings. I knew that the market for such an invention was potentially huge.

To those of you who have not searched for gels in plastics, a little background briefing may be in order. When most plastics are cool and solid they are not very transparent. But when almost all plastics are molten, if they do not contain fillers or colorants, they become transparent. I knew that most plastics processing is done as part of the extruding or molding process. Therefore, the logical place to detect plastic gels would be within the plastics machinery.

But I still did not know how to see the gels, even in fairly clear molten plastic, because the gels are tiny. A gel is usually smaller than a pinhead and is floating around in a very hostile environment of high pressures and temperatures, strong chemicals and fumes, and other obstacles. It needed more thought on my part.

Step 2 – Preliminary product concept
I had only a vague idea about how to "see" the gels in molten plastic. An optical approach seemed most promising. What I needed was some sort of very robust probe that would allow for a remote vision on a micro scale into molten plastic. What I was considering was like finding a way to use field glasses to look into a live volcano. It was a challenge, and I set out to solve it.

Then one of those little miracles of inspiration happened. While walking at dawn in the mountainous countryside in upstate New York, I chanced to see dewdrops glittering on a spider's web. That's when it hit me. The light was sparkling from the dewdrops like the sparkles of light from a chandelier.

Sunlight shining from the other side of the tiny dewdrops causes them to shine brilliantly as points of light even in the considerable early morning mist.

Furthermore, the vibration of the dew drops in the gentle morning breezes made them shimmer and glitter, so that they stood out even more from their background. This "shimmering" insight would be the key to success in the product development. As an engineer I saw that an optical concept had presented itself. I could now develop an instrument that would allow tiny impurities to be seen in murky molten plastic. It could not only detect gels but probably count them as well. I was elated by my discovery and anxious to get to work on it.

My vision of a polymer gel detection instrument was sparked by the optics of a spider web in the first rays of the sun.

Step 3 - Let's start a company!
By the time I returned to my home in New Jersey, I had mapped out both the preliminary design of the product as well as the form and structure of the company I would need to commercialize it. I estimated that at least a million dollars would be needed to bankroll the new venture. A positive factor was that I managed a small plastics machinery company. I could do some initial new product development within this company, and I was known to be an effective general manager.

I knew I had to develop a working prototype. I would also have to apply for a patent, develop prospective customer interest, and then talk to prospective investors. I had found a potential product concept. Now I had to work towards starting a new company. I knew a major investment of time and money would be needed.

Papers were drawn up to form the new company to commercialize my new product, but the new company had no staff, facilities or finance. Yet the idea of a new company seemed to be a *fait accompli*. The details would be attended to when I had a business plan and the company's needs became clearer. Meanwhile, the product development project was carried out within the plastics machinery company that I managed.

Step 4 - Product development
I settled into the exciting and adventurous work of product development. It took many nights and weekends. For months, I found myself experimenting with various combinations of electronics and optics to "see" the pinhead-size gels in molten plastic.

I needed to illuminate the gels. The most promising technique was one I borrowed from medical endoscope technology.

Used by doctors, fiber optic bundles are snaked into the body to see magnified images of interior body parts. I would use a similar process employing a highly protected magnifying lens at the end of a protected fiber optic bundle. I needed a fiber optic bundle on the other side of the plastic melt flow connected to an intense light source. The result would be that the gels would be illuminated the way the early morning sun had illuminated the dewdrops on the spider's web.

Once the plastic was illuminated, the images of the gels were converted to video. This made automated image analysis possible. Next, I had to figure out how to see the gels moving in a flow channel without the confusion of static artifacts in the channel. The quavering motion of dewdrops makes them stand out much more distinctly from the background. I decided to program the electronics to detect only moving gels so that the static artifacts would not be seen.

Motion detection would come from special video circuitry developed for surveillance and security used for detecting intruders in an otherwise quiet parking lot. To accomplish this, all of the fiber optics and lens systems had to be specially designed to withstand temperatures of up to 800 degrees F (427 degrees C) and pressures of thousands of pounds per square inch.

I purchased experimental equipment as components: a second-hand video camera and monitor from a war surplus store, fiber optics endoscopes from a medical supply house, and other bits and pieces from wherever they could be found. It was all very crude, but when everything was connected together, it sort-of worked. A little vision, a lot of bargain hunting, and imagination still helped!

My employees and I started simply. We looked at grit particles in water. Then we graduated to grit particles in Jell-O.

Finally, we arrived at grit particles in molten plastic. Then we improved our equipment and technique so that we could see the tiny transparent gels in the almost transparent molten plastic. With the video image enhancement, the gels appeared as bright round blobs much like micrographs of blood cells. Eureka! I found it!

To make the gel imaging instrument useful, it also had to size and count the gels in the polymer flow channel. Therefore, by the time we had a demonstration instrument ready for the first prospective customers, it also incorporated a homemade image analysis computer to size and count the moving gels. That computer used sophisticated artificial intelligence algorithms to substitute for a human in dynamic image analysis although we were only vaguely aware of the new science of AI at that time.

The machine stood almost three feet high and was about a foot and a half wide and a foot and a half deep. It was crammed with electronics. The estimated manufacturing cost of the complete gel detecting and counting instrument was about $30,000. My proposed sales price was $78,500. (Never mind about by what mystical process I arrived at that price except that I do recall it netted a profit margin that is typical for industrial instrumentation.)

By now, a year after the initial product conception, our development team consisted of me as the electronic engineer, a consulting polymer chemist, a mechanical engineer, and a consulting software development group. We were all paid by the plastics machinery company I managed because as a new venture we had not yet raised outside financing.

We needed some market feedback before we invested further in product development. What would they think about my new product in the plastics production plants?

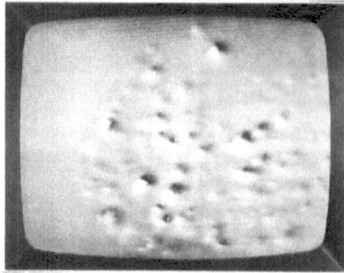

Gel detection instrument above left in our plastics extrusion laboratory, Flow Vision, Inc., Clifton, New Jersey, 1985. An instrument video of gels in the polymer melt stream is shown to the left. The gels are about the diameter of a human hair.

Step 5 - First Encounters with the market

Our encounters with the market threw us into a prolonged funk. Who would want to buy one of our gel counters at $78,500? Certainly, the average plastics products plant that made cups or plastic bags could not afford it. We wondered where all this hard work had taken us. Perhaps it was just an expensive science project. Maybe my vision had propelled us into uncharted territory where we really did not want to go. We were approaching Christmas, and there were few prospects of tidings of great joy. I thought that I would soon have to shelve the project and concentrate our dwindling resources on our traditional plastics machinery business. It was lower tech, lower profit potential, but a relatively reliable and steady business.

Then the phone rang. I could not believe my ears. The man on the other end of the line said that they would buy an instrument if we could deliver by year-end—about 20 days away. It was Dow Chemical in Texas calling. They had seen a brief description of our product in a trade magazine new product publicity release. Their plastics were shipped in pellet form by the railcar load to the people who make plastic bags and a wide variety of other household products. They had a serious gel problem, and it was affecting the million or so pounds of raw polyethylene plastic they were producing each day.

The catch was that any leftover project funds at Dow were available only if they were spent on goods delivered by year-end. This is common practice in larger companies and government agencies. Our salvation came because someone at Dow did not want to send the funds back to the corporate coffers! We accepted the order without any real hope of completing the instrument on time. You can guess what we were doing on Christmas day.

Word got around. We sold a second instrument to Dow. (We guessed the first one had performed well. Dow generally did not hand out accolades.) Soon after, DuPont bought one to ensure fiber quality control for bulk nylon production. An engineer from Exxon Chemicals appeared one day, and the following day there was an order for an instrument to do research analysis of synthetic rubber production. We had found our market or, more accurately, the market had found us. The market was in bulk plastic production, known in the trade as polymer and fiber production.

>>> *With innovative new products, very often you do not know
what the real market segment or customer category will be. Do
not be blinded by your initial perception of who the typical customer will be, and allow time for the true market to present itself.*

Step 6 - Looking for finance

It was time to start looking for serious investment money. Up
to now, our operating funds came from the plastics machinery company I managed. Our new venture was conceived
as the machinery company's research project. Additional
funding came in as small amounts of "friends' and relatives'" money—typically investments of $5,000-$20,000. But
in order to purchase laboratory and production equipment,
build a starting product inventory, cover salaries and traveling expenses and so on, we needed much larger investments of "serious money." All of those expenditures were
estimated to add up to about a half million dollars. This
amount of investment called for very wealthy individuals
called "angels" or venture capital, which is investment by
professional investment firms. We were in the greater New
York City area. Plentiful investment capital can be searched
out there, but the process can be as daunting as inventing
and developing the product.

Then I stumbled upon a timely and fortuitous circum-
stance. It was spring, and I was taking my fiancee on a drive
out to the beaches on Long Island. In Southampton, which is a
traditional bastion of "old money," we stopped at a huge white
classical house set among great lawns and spreading trees. This
mansion had been my great grandfather's house. He had been
a flamboyant financier until the Great Depression hit, when he
was forced to sell and move in to a modest "cottage" nearby.
The mansion had been designed by the famous architect,

Stanford White, who was one of my great grandfather's close friends.

My mother had told me stories of sneaking a peek at their boisterous parties from upstairs in the big house. Nude girls would jump from a huge pie or cake. One of those girls had been Evelyn Nesbit, the "girl on the red velvet swing," whose insanely jealous husband later murdered Stanford White.

By the time I was showing my fiancee around the grounds, the house had been purchased by some real estate developers who had renovated it and turned it into a 20-unit condominium. We peeked into a condominium apartment made from what had once been the billiard room. The owner appeared, a pleasant portly fellow from South Africa. He introduced us to his French fiancee from the Riviera. He was fascinated to meet a descendant of the house's original owner. He was also intrigued when I told him about the plastics gel counter—a saga I managed to weave into the end of my summary of family history. From out of the blue he allowed as how he might be interested in investing in my new company if I could present it to his associated investment banking firm, Drexel Burnham Lambert in Manhattan.

I could not believe my luck! I never expected to be introduced to that sacred temple of new enterprise finance, let alone by a casual visit to Southampton. Drexel Burnham, as it was called, was a large and growing investment banking firm famous for investing in larger companies with low-quality (usually unsecured) "junk bonds." But Drexel Burnham also had a small venture capital group specializing in placing client funds in start-up companies just like mine. This group, called the Lambda Funds, showed a lot of interest when I enthusiastically described the new company, its product, its prospects, and its goals, after I had been introduced by the gentleman from South Africa. They were particularly captivated by my vision, I suspect, because they had no technical basis to evaluate the venture in the first meetings. That was all right with me. A month later they decided to invest $500,000.

>>> *If there is a lesson in this episode, I think it might be "breach the walls of the financial world wherever you can." Once you are inside the inner sanctum, one introduction leads to another and, with a good vision and a reasonable business plan to offset it, money may well follow.*

Step 7 - Organizing the company

With this momentum established, I decided to call my company Flow Vision because its product represented a way to see the microscopic gels in polymer flowing by a viewing port. I feel that a company name should relate to your product and be short and easily remembered. Remember, if your company grows and prospers, its name will evolve into the all-important brand. By then if you have picked an unmemorable name, it is too late to change it.

An artist introduced by our publicity advisor made us up a nice logo. We felt like we were right up there with the big boys. I asked everyone who might be "in the know" to recommend a good patent attorney. I needed one with a strong engineering background because of the technical nature of the enterprise. The one I found told us that we probably would be receiving a patent that would be "strong", because it would be based on more than minor variations of existing techniques. (For a further and more detailed discussion of patents see Chapter three).

I also made a videotape showing the gels flowing by in the molten plastic. It was black and white with no sound, but it mesmerized the prospective investors. The investors were told about millions of pairs of panty hose that would not have runs in them, and milk jugs that would no longer leak because the gels that caused the runs and leaks would be eliminated. The video was tangible proof of my vision. With this atmosphere of success, I made additional presentations on Wall Street. We raised another half million dollars from two investment firms, bringing the total venture capital investment in Flow Vision to a million dollars.

What we had was a magical combination of novel product, a patent pending, an apparently unlimited market, and a few orders from the polymer raw material giants. The original vision was still carrying us forward. Goals for the business had been established in the financial terms that the investors could relate to. Everyone was feeling very pleased. Excitement was mounting at the expectation of new achievements.

Flow Vision grew according to plan for a few years. On paper, I was a forty-year-old multimillionaire. Then everything began to dissolve. A recession hit and the polymer industry tanked. Suddenly the big companies were buying only "necessary" items, like forklift trucks and personal computers. Quality control equipment, such as ours, would have to wait.

I became despondent. My investors said that I had "lost the vision". They demanded that the shrinking business be sold while it still had some market value. Just then a defense electronics company came along and purchased our company as a commercial diversification, essentially for salvage value. I knew then how my great grandfather the financier had felt when he realized he had to move from the mansion to the cottage.

After a few years of regaining perspective and getting new ideas, I recovered and started a new company, Eco Sensors, Inc. This has been a great success, as we shall see later in this book.

Will Your Vision Lead to a Viable Business?

Knowing in advance that you have a viable product, good employees, and investors to back up your vision does not guarantee a business ultimate success. You cannot forecast a major recession years before it happens. What you can do is be flexible enough to deal with setbacks as well as the opportunities, as they arise.

In thinking about Flow Vision, I have not been able to think of any one thing that we could have done to have assured more success. We could have remained part of the plastics machinery company with modest or no outside financing. We then would not have fallen as hard during the recession. But the plastics machinery parent company was itself sliding down the slippery slope of continuing losses in an intensely competitive industry. Probably we should have sold ourselves as a technology package to a DuPont or a Dow. The buyer then could have had an exclusive method to increase their product quality.

In my first visionary business, making polymer quality analyzers, customers showed up to buy our products only in the good times. I now realize that they considered our product to be an expensive non-necessity. In a way, we were an "intriguing engineering project". Perhaps the most important question you should always return to is "I have a great product, but is it an absolute necessity or a fun gadget?"

Gleaning Opportunity from Failure

The vision for my second company and my personal salvation started with my first company's customers. I had often heard: "Why are you making instruments that monitor the manufacturing process, when we are spending the big bucks on environmental monitoring?" It was true. The polymer chemical industry had stopped major additional spending for manufacturing improvement. Instead, it was spending discretionary dollars for equipment that dealt with environmental issues.

I started designing and then manufacturing simple instruments to monitor hydrocarbon emissions. But that market application was very competitive, and sales were disappointing. Then one day a customer said: "Do you realize that your hydrocarbon instrument works great for detecting ozone?" I was not really sure what ozone was, but I have since found out that it appears in countless processes and activities. I redirected the business to concentrate on making the world's simplest and most inexpensive ozone monitors.

Eco Sensors seemed like a good name for this new business. People showed up from all kinds of unexpected places to buy my monitors. I readily will admit that in my second business the vision was not as dramatic as it was for my first business, but the products have more value for a broader market. There is more basis for a real business.

I started this business very small so that I could finance it myself. I designed the circuits myself and soldered components to the experimental prototype boards on the dining room table in my wife's family's cabin on a lake in New York's Catskill Mountains. A photo of the homemade first instrument next to a production version is shown in chapter eight.

I paid myself a living wage so that I could reinvest most of the earnings to finance the company's growth. (The IRS says, incidentally, that you the owner must pay yourself a reasonable salary. They want your payroll taxes.). I was worth over a million again. This time there were no investors to argue with. My vision for the company changed from time to time, but I did not have to justify these revised visions to anybody. I might add that my wife and my employees said that I was easier to get along with.

In late 2007 I sold Eco Sensors to KWJ Engineering in the San Francisco Bay area. They are a larger company whose much stronger research and development department has been developing gas sensing technologies that I could not do at Eco Sensors. I joined their board, where I can lend my experience and insights to everyone's benefit.

In the chapters that follow, I will try to help you build a solid foundation under your vision. We are going to explore how to take specific action to go from having a great idea to forming a great company that works for you.

2

DEVELOP A PRODUCT

Everything new is resisted.
Thomas A. Edison

There is no set formula for finding or developing a product line. First, as we saw in the last chapter, being alert and opportunistic is a must. The new product insight can appear unexpectedly, just as my polymer idea did when I saw the spider's web. Second, find something that will hold your interest through the tough years of start-up. Your pride in your product and your belief in its value can carry you through the evenings and weekends of development and company start-up. Third, try to find something that is "Just slightly ahead of our time," as the very successful electronics company, Panasonic, puts it. Anticipate people's needs, but try to keep away from advances in technology that become endless development projects.

Take your time and proceed slowly. Do not worry about developing all the products you might need in five years. You will find that the more successful you become, the more additional product ideas will come your way, whether you ask for them or not. Additional products for later stages of the business will tend to emerge in the flow of events. Begin with something that will be the basis for your successful business. Hopefully, this modest start will establish your reputation and your brand name.

Considerations in Selecting a Product Line

Whether you start with someone else's products or with your own, always start with products that fit within your own business experience and abilities. It may sound like fun to run a bed & breakfast, but will the less glamorous aspects of that business, like constantly fixing the plumbing in that charming old house, cool your ardor for being an innkeeper? Maybe a mail order business sounds intriguing. Perhaps you have envisioned yourself shipping wine cellar accessories to the rich and the famous all over the world. But, for instance, did you know that 90% of all mail order businesses is customer list management using sophisticated computer techniques? The bottom line with mail order houses is to increase the order rate on one million-plus mailings. It is in these high numbers that the profits are made. Even though you may be a wine connoisseur, it may have little effect on the success of a mail order wine accessory business.

This might be a good time to sit down and consider the things you do well and enjoy doing. Ask yourself the following questions:

- Do you inspire and manage people well?
- Do you enjoy dealing with the public?
- Do you like to work with computers and software?
- Can you create and develop products or works of art?

- Are you good at dealing with overseas customers or suppliers?
- Do you have in-depth specialty knowledge such as banking, machinery manufacturing, flower growing, or data transmission?
- _____? (You fill it in.)

You may not realize how much of these attributes are passed along through family influences and long-standing relationships with friends. Our family over several generations has always excelled in making things, so we have developed products and businesses in oil burners, machinery, bird feeders, gift cards, and electronic instruments. On the other hand, we have never had a knack for real estate. Get to know your strong points and be ready to muster them for your new enterprise. Also, be honest with yourself about the areas you do not excel in so that you can make the best choices for your new business.

Acquiring a Product Line

When you have decided what business you would like to be in, you can consider the best way to acquire the business' starting product line (a group or range of products for the same market segment or application).

Let's say you would like to start a commercial sign painting shop. You could acquire the rights to a franchise in your area which specializes in commercial sign painting. In return for a substantial franchise fee, you can receive a complete package of know-how, supplies, equipment, specialty software, advertising packages, training at the home office, and more. On the other hand, you could start your own sign painting service with less financial outlay, but you might make less without the professional support of the franchise organization. Advertisements for various franchise opportunities are found in entrepreneurial magazines among other sources.

Perhaps you think there is a big and unfulfilled market for a plant food which is organically correct and non-toxic. After researching the field, you might find out there is a chemical formulation used in a foreign country but not in use here. Plan to make a short vacation trip to that country, visit the product's owners, and see if you can get the rights to import it and sell it here. With any luck, they might let you package the product under your own brand name. Many years ago, I met a man who had tremendous success with just such a foreign product. He had found a funny little economical car while vacationing in Germany. Just for asking, he received the Volkswagen of America franchise! If you've got a good eye, on the other hand, when considering the plant food business, if you know about biology and chemistry, you might develop your own "proprietary" formulation. ("Proprietary" means the formulation is your own design and usually means that the formulation is secret or patented. I will discuss proprietary information management in the next chapter.)

Another way to acquire a product line is to buy one from an existing company. I have done this when I bought a line of quality control inspection equipment. This equipment complemented my existing inspection products and so could be offered to my customers at little additional sales cost. You can often find a good product line at a bargain price if the current owner has a business which is either shifting its focus or is in financial trouble. You can usually get product designs, drawings, parts or ingredient lists, inventory, patents (if there are any), the right to the product name, customer lists, and often a person called the "product manager."

These product line acquisitions are often well worth seeking out. You are buying not only a product line but also a business, often at much less than it would cost you to do it. Often you can work out an installment payment plan. In that case the seller will more than likely want some cash up front. You will also need cash for starting capital. If you decide to take this approach, think in terms of spending at least $100,000 to start-up. You should also seek the counsel of a good business lawyer because product line acquisition agreements typically include many considerations you may not be aware of.

The difficulty in acquiring product lines is that they are hard to find. They are often not published or advertised as being available, even in their own industry. They can best be found by talking to people in the industry that interests you. A good way to visit with all the companies in your target industry is by touring the industry's leading trade show. Often, a company's president or other senior officers will be in their exhibit booth.

Most of my experience and the experience of my family have been in creating or inventing products. Therefore, I am going to concentrate on this approach in what follows. I will also be highlighting generalities to bear in mind, no matter what the source of your products.

Inventing Your Own Products

It is hard to believe that even Thomas Edison thought that the inventor's life was a tough one. Nevertheless, an innovative new product is still one of the best ways to make a fortune from scratch. What you have to do is to adjust your attitude so you can persevere over a long and bumpy road. There will be a few intriguing discoveries to pump you up along the way and many more details to overcome. You do not have to be a genius to be a successful inventor or a new product developer. As Edison himself observed: "Genius is 1% inspiration and 99% perspiration."

Product design is probably easier today than in Edison's day. Edison might have had a better shot at developing a fundamental new product that could change everyone's life, like the light bulb, but you have the opportunity to develop one or more of a thousand potential new applications of light. Just think of all the products that are being developed from fiber optics. This technology was a key part of my plastics quality analyzer and its company, Flow Vision. Whatever your area you do not need to be a technical expert to develop a new product. There is probably an opportunity to create a better dog's dish or cat litter box without being an engineer. You just have to understand the world of dogs or cats and be willing to look at things from a fresh perspective. It is heartening to remind yourself that the market for pet products today is much larger than the market for light bulbs was in Edison's day.

How do you start in the product development process? It is almost always better to perfect a simple product than to never finish the development of something more complex. As a general guideline, look for a very simple development unless you have a lot more resources in terms of people, equipment and funding than the average start-up business. Other key points to keep in mind are:

- Look for a simple but attractive improvement to enhance an existing product type. My father redesigned existing wooden bird feeders. He created more attractive and functional plastic bird feeders and made a small fortune.

- Think about product design in terms of appearance and simplicity. I built a great business making gas detection instruments. My designs are better looking and have fewer switches, buttons, and other controls than the competition. My instruments are cheaper than even Asian competitors.
- Look for the connectedness of everything. You can combine mechanical and electrical concepts, cooking, kitchen management, and who knows what else to come up with the world's first really good bagel toaster. Engineers, scientists, and academics may despair when asked to analyze anything with many apparently unrelated variables, but it is perfectly okay for you to do this in pursuit of a new product.
- Do experiments, no matter how crude and imperfect, to improve your insights and understanding so that you can move forward with your product design.
- Don't worry about what other people think or say. Keep observing and hold on to your vision.

Refining Your Product

Experience shows that time is hardly ever wasted if it is invested in product development and refinement at the earliest stages of a new company. Later you will have a lot less time to allocate to product development. Keep in mind that once your fledgling business has begun to build up significant good will with your customers, it is a shame to throw it away with a generation of products that do not work. I have found that customers have very long memories for disappointing products.

>>> *No matter what product you set out to develop, do intense product and business developments before you formally approach*

potential investors or business associates. Every improvement in your product design, every step further in market development, and all other advances of the business, will be to your advantage in negotiating with your first investors and associates.

Case study
The Maestro Develops a Bird Feeder

My father's persistence in working towards product perfection has been an inspiration to me. His work taught me that even something of apparent simplicity, like a bird feeder, is worth the full development effort.

Well into his 50s, my father sold his last machinery business. By that time he had had several technically satisfying but financially marginal businesses. He seemed bogged down and going no-where. One rainy day, while feeling despondent, he was looking out a window at a bird feeder swinging in the breeze. It had no birds on it. It was a design, popular at the time, where there was a small rustic round wooden log, about two inches in diameter and about a foot long. Eight one-inch diameter holes were drilled into the log, where peanut butter or suet bird food could be placed. At the time, these feeders were very popular with people, but they were not especially popular with the birds.

My father began to think about designing a bird feeder that would be mass-producible yet also be a hit with the birds. The basic idea in the existing design of the vertical feeders was that peanut butter or suet would be troweled into the holes. My father knew a greater variety of interesting birds preferred seeds to peanut butter or suet. His first breakthrough was to think of the feeder as a hollow tube holding seeds instead of a log with holes drilled in it.

My father found the vertical tube design, with perches at feedholes, to be a better starting point than the log. If the feeder could be made of clear plastic tubing, moreover, the birds could see the seeds in it. The feeder could also be easily filled by pouring the seeds in through the top. Shiny metal caps on top and bottom and metal perches would make the bird feeder both stylish and easily manufacturable.

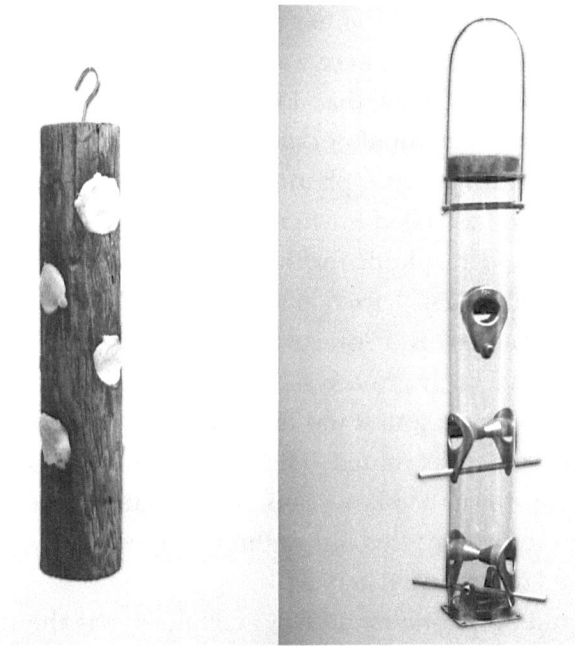

Bird feeder improvement. My father Peter Kilham's plastic and metal design was a great advance over the traditional wooden feeder. 1969.

Still the question that had to be answered was: "What will the birds think of the new feeder?" My father hung several bird feeders outside of his kitchen window to find out. He was determined to keep experimenting, after studying the birds' reactions to each design change. He had that twinkle in his eyes when he told me: "When they're dissatisfied the birds scold; when they're pleased their notes almost sound like applause."

My father tried all sorts of things to please the birds. He found that the perch rods were very important. He tried non-slip toe grips. His wife Dorothy, who was secretary of the business, gave him letters from early customers of the feeders. They were concerned that on cold winter days the birds' feet could freeze to the metal perches. There was a lot of discussion, worry and experimentation about this. Eventually my father concluded that the birds' feet would not stick even on the coldest days.

I was working in the plastics industry at the time, and so my expertise was called for to deal with another problem. We needed to select a plastic for the clear tube serving as the bird feeder's body. First, I tried polystyrene. This was an obvious choice because it is a low-cost basic industrial plastic, available in crystal clear grades, such as those used for disposable "glasses." What we found was that after a few weeks in the sun the polystyrene was ruined. The ultraviolet energy of the sunlight broke down the plastic causing it to "craze" all over. I used additives to prevent this but nothing helped. The same thing happened when I tried acrylic.

Butyrate, a plastic made from cellulose, was the next candidate. It was not as readily available as the other plastics I had tried, but it seemed more stable in our outdoor tests. Then there was a jolting discovery: the squirrels loved it! They chewed it up like candy, probably savoring the salt in it.

Finally we turned our attention to polycarbonate, often known by one of its trade names, Lexan®. Actually, we were aware of polycarbonate from the beginning, but we were dragging our feet in trying it because it was both more costly (over twice the cost of the other common plastics), and it was also more difficult to process. The company I managed at the time manufactured plastics machinery, so I knew how the polycarbonate should be extruded. I knew it required much higher temperatures and pressures than most other common plastics. But there was no getting around it. The polycarbonate worked beautifully. It was crystal clear, did not scratch easily, was not affected by the sun, and seemed distasteful to the squirrels.

>>> *In selecting kinds and grades of materials for a product design it pays big dividends to try many types and grades until you are really satisfied with the appearance and performance of the product. Potential suppliers are often very helpful with their engineering assistance, but it is unlikely that they will have the insight about your application or your customers that you should be developing through your own experimentation.*

The most persistent problem of the new bird feeder designs was the squirrels. They could shinny up the slick support poles planted in the ground to hold the feeders. They could drop down from swaying tree branches. They could leap over from almost anywhere. We tried everything to keep them off the feeders. One solution which worked was to put an old black phonograph record above the feeder (for hanging feeders) or below the feeder (for pole feeders). The birds did not mind the records. In fact, they seemed pleased that the squirrels were not stealing their meal. Later there were specially designed molded polycarbonate squirrel guards, but personally I think the records worked best.

My father sold his first bird feeders through local feed and garden stores. The birds had not been officially heard from, but in a few months, bird experts pronounced the feeders bird-friendly.

One gratifying result was that the National Audubon Society stocked them in all their gift shops. Unfortunately, only a tiny minority of the shopping public visits these places. My father knew he had a successful new feeder, but at the rate they were selling it would take years to mass-market the feeders.

Then my father heard about a distributor who was a specialist in home and garden specialty items. The distributor said he would market test the bird feeders at an upcoming trade show in New York. To everyone's astonishment the distributor received orders at his trade show booth for 16,000 feeders. That was equivalent to one year's sales. Word got around. Executives of distributors and stores, some of whom never had even thought about birds before, flew like homing pigeons to my father's place in a backwater New England town to negotiate sales agreements.

Essential to my father's bird feeder success was an established market that was very susceptible to a better product design. Even though he did not know the size of the bird feeder market, he could see that the existing bird feeder designs could use improvement. He knew it was important to design a product that was mass-producible at low cost, using local manufacturing contractors. He had had a previous business where he did much of his own manufacturing, and he had found that the personnel and financial problems associated with manufacturing were overwhelming.

Because of his know-how, the time to success for his bird feeder business was only about two years. This is considered a very short time for a new product. Three years is often cited as the expected amount of time to break-even for a small business.

An interesting footnote to the bird feeder business was that its sales tended to be opposite of the health of the economy. Apparently, during bad times, people buy bird feeders to cheer themselves up by watching the ever-perky birds outside. On Wall Street they call this a "counter-cyclical play."

Although my father, Peter Kilham, has passed away, its employees, to whom it was bequeathed, are carrying on the tradition of his company, Droll Yankees®, Inc. A new tool they have brought to its marketing success is a great Web site on the Internet, www.drollyankees.com where you can see his picture, the bird feeders, and new developments for attracting our backyard friends. Peter Kilham was interested in innovating in all aspects of a business, and I am sure he would have quickly seized the Web marketing opportunity.

My father, Peter Kilham, surrounded by his bird feeders in his shop at Droll Yankees, Inc. in Foster, Rhode Island, in the 1980s.

Building a Castle with a Wall of Patents

The oil burner business

In my grandfather's time, the cost of patents, including patent attorney fees and all other expenses, was less than in my father's time and much less than today. A patent can cost $8,000 or more today. Back when patents were cheap, my grandfather, James "Jim" L. Breese, Jr., had an oil burner business based on over 100 patents he accumulated over his lifetime. After patenting a basic oil burner design, he would patent improvements to the design, and improvements to the improvements. This defensive approach is called a "patent fence" and has helped protect the proprietary advantage of many large technology companies.

My grandfather's design improvements tended to revolve around the electronic controls he developed for the oil burners. The importance of these controls to providing a product advantage proved to be the main value of the business in its final years.

Over about 20 years, he developed oil burners for use in home furnaces, water heaters, and light commercial and military applications. These were the "pot" type design where the oil flows into a stainless steel pot and burns via hundreds of combustion holes around the sides of the pot. In the 1930s through the 1950s, millions of these burners were sold, and my grandfather collected royalties from other companies who had agreements with him to manufacture and sell them. The income from royalties based on his patent fence gave him a good income for many years.

Of course, just cranking out more patents was not all that was required to develop the business. Sometimes, for example, dramatic demonstrations were helpful. For some time the military had been using his pot-type burner for field stoves. A complication arose, however. The military wanted to standardize on only one fuel for all field equipment so they selected gasoline instead of stocking both gasoline and fuel oil. A point in my grandfather's favor was that gasoline does not work well in the gun-type burners (the new technology that was beginning to replace pot-type oil burners) because it does not provide enough lubrication for the bearings, and they soon burn out.

However, as his son, Jim, recalled, "Of course there was a lot of official resistance to the idea of burning gasoline. The Corps of Engineers types at Ft. Belvoir visualized cataclysmic explosions, and a colonel from there flew out to discuss the matter with Dad. They sat next to a Jerry can full of gasoline while Dad tried to explain that liquid gasoline doesn't explode. Then he lit a cigarette and tossed the burning match into the open can. The colonel, white as a ghost, hit the dirt. But of course the match fizzled, and the point was made."

Timing and market acceptance must be considered equally along with product perfection. In his final years, my grandfather was still designing oil burners. Bed-ridden, he would send sketches via a faithful assistant to his model shop as ideas for experimental design improvements. Unfortunately, this effort was doomed to be futile because the pot-type burner was rapidly being displaced by the gun-type oil burner and by natural gas heating.

We all live in different times and confront different threats to the creations in our business. In the next chapter I will discuss a variety of techniques you could employ in your emerging business to protect your great ideas.

*My grandfather, James L. Breese, Jr., working
on a new oil burner in his outdoor lab at Breese
Burners, Inc. Santa Fe, New Mexico, 1950.*

3

PROTECTING YOUR PRODUCT PATENTS, TRADEMARKS, COPYRIGHTS AND TRADE SECRETS

An ounce of prevention...

You have come up with a great product idea and a great business name and logo. Now, how are you going to protect them?

Entrepreneurs starting businesses based on innovative products, inventions, and works of art have always been very concerned about protection of their intellectual property. For over a hundred years, extensive commercial law has developed addressing patents, trademarks, copyrights and trade secrets. This is a very legalistic area and so at the earliest stages you should find a good patent and trademark attorney and review your developments and plans with him or her. In this chapter, I will only try to address practical business considerations that should greatly enhance your chances for success.

Suppose you develop a better can opener, and you would like to build a business based on it. You do not want your ideas exploited by competitors, and you do not want your new business' name, ideas, slogans and the like copied. What can you do? You can:

- Patent the can opener if its design is truly novel. Patenting can be litigious and costly. (I will discuss this further later in this chapter.)
- Trademark the product. Beginners often overlook the power of a good trademark in business. Even though there are pitfalls to this approach, if you do your homework carefully, you can effectively protect much of your business with a simple trademark.
- Secure copyrights. Copyrights are applicable in more areas than just the obvious ones such as works of art. They can also protect your technical writings and software.
- Protect your trade secrets. You will be surprised to find out how much of your design, manufacturing know-how and knowledge of niche markets would-be competitors do not know about. Keeping trade secrets can therefore be good business protection.

The problem for the start-up small business is that carrying out all or many of these protective measures to the extent recommended by experts can be expensive and very time-consuming. Everything must be examined for pitfalls and kept in perspective.

Protecting Trade Secrets

You will have all kinds of special information that gives your business a competitive edge. You may develop this information yourself or you may acquire it through a franchise agreement or product license. In any case, as time goes on, you will be developing proprietary information (also referred to as "intellectual property") which must be protected.

Industrial espionage such as portrayed in the movies may happen once in a great while, but most often proprietary information walks out the door with a departing employee. Therefore, many businesses have their employees sign non-compete agreements. These are useful because they indicate to the new employee that you will not take information stealing lightly.

The problem is that these agreements are often watered down or even thrown out by the courts. In the United States public policy tends to favor granting employees the right to work where they choose and to pursue their trade or profession regardless of any past employment agreements.

Without getting into all the legal whereofs and wherefors, which are endless on this subject, here are the precautions that I have found to be helpful:

Be careful with employment agreements
Be specific and reasonable about the non-compete conditions. The business area should be limited to the products and services described in your brochures. Stating in your agreement that the employee cannot compete in making can openers is probably okay, but requesting a non-compete agreement for general household appliances will not hold up in court. The non-compete agreement can extend out to about three years. If it is longer, most courts will strike the clause as unreasonable. The following extract from my company's employment agreement illustrates the point:

In return for the above compensation package as a full-time employee of Eco Sensors, Inc. you agree:

1 - Not to compete in the field VOC and ozone gas sensing monitoring for a period of three years after leaving Eco Sensors, Inc. employment.

2 - You agree that all patents, proprietary developments, and customer lists become the property of Eco Sensors, Inc. as they are developed.

Identify proprietary information and policy

Indicate to employees, contractors, distributors and suppliers what is proprietary information. Make sure everyone recognizes that proprietary information and its protection is your company's policy. The courts are more likely to sympathize with you as the employer if the purloined information was known to be proprietary and worthy of protection. Be sure to spell out your proprietary information protection policies in your company policy manual or employee handbook, if you have one. The courts tend to respect policy manuals if they are reasonable.

Compartmentalize proprietary information

It is fine to talk about sales with the engineers and general developments in engineering with the salespeople, but be careful. The salespeople, however nice they may be, have no need to know where you buy that special little part that makes yours the world's best can opener, and the engineers do not need to have access to your customer lists either. Of course, an engineer and a salesperson could leave together to start a competing business, but there is no need to make their job any easier by giving away your proprietary information.

Make your product hard to copy

I always assume that potential competitors will buy samples of my product on the open market. There is nothing I can do to prevent this. What I can do is to delay their development process, which when they buy a finished product and try to imitate it, is known as "reverse engineering." For my electronic products, we remove part numbers from critical semiconductor chips on the circuit board. The bad guys may figure out the identity of the chips eventually, but we may have delayed them by at least a few months. When you are creating your product, look for ways to make your manufacturing process hard to trace.

Use confidential disclosure agreements

Confidential disclosure agreements, generally known as "non-disclosure agreements" or "NDCs," are widely used when promoting early versions of high tech and complex products. Your prospective customer needs to try out your product. Key suppliers also need to see how to integrate their parts with your product. To prevent these early users from becoming competitors, consider having them sign non-disclosure agreements.

These agreements have a defined validity period—usually three to five years. They specify a specified product or technology (whether or not the technology is patented). Non-disclosure agreements normally become invalidated when the protected technology becomes public knowledge. If you use such agreements, review the wording and provisions carefully to avoid hidden loopholes.

You may get sample non-disclosure agreements from business friends, especially if they are in technology-based companies, or from an Internet search. A business lawyer, however, should review your proposed standard agreement.

Designate authority for proprietary information transmittal
Have all requests for proprietary information which come into your business pass through you. Such a request, perhaps one from a parts supplier, however innocent sounding, can be part of a process of building up an information file about your product or business. If all these requests go through you, you will be able to sense a pattern developing. Then you can be on the alert for a new competitor.

Trademarks

In many ways, a trademark is the simplest and often most effective protection you can get. A trademark is a broad term that applies to any word, name, symbol or device that manufacturers and merchants use to identify and distinguish goods and services. Even though you do not have to register a trademark to use it, you should register it as soon as possible and in all the important market countries and the business expands. A patent and trademark attorney should do the actual registrations.

Because trademarks do not have to be registered, there is no foolproof way of finding out if a trademark is in use. What you can do is to review the suitability of a proposed trademark by discussing it with experienced people in the business, looking for its use in trade publications, and searching state and national trademark reference guides, which can be found both in libraries and on the Web.

When I was studying at MIT, I took a patent course taught by a famous patent attorney, Robert Rhines. He was patent counsel to several major electronic companies. Professor Rhines told us his favorite story about the Sylvania Blue Dot camera flash bulbs.

At that time, Sylvania (now a division of GTE Corporation) was a leading producer of camera flash bulbs. In those days, flash bulbs could only be used once. Often they had air leaks and would not flash. The Sylvania engineers invented a blue chemical dot that was put inside the bulb during the manufacturing process so that the consumer could be assured that the bulb would work before attempting to use it. This dot would be destroyed by air leaking into the bulb. If the photographer saw that there was no blue dot, he or she knew that the bulb would not flash and needed to be replaced.

Flash bulb sales increased dramatically even though it turned out that hardly anyone knew what the purpose of the blue dot was. The blue dot had become a trademark that people associated with quality.

Trademarks are registered in each country where you want the trademark to have legal protection. Usually you must show that your trademark has been in commercial use. This can be done by showing a sample of your brochures and business documents displaying the trademark. Most countries will not accept generic trademarks. *Super Can Opener* probably will not pass muster as a trademark but *Kitchen King* probably will. If you have not registered your trademark, you put a TM after it; if you have registered it you should use the circle R sign ® instead.

To illustrate the importance courts attach to trademarks, I recall an interesting case when I was working for a medical laboratory equipment company. We manufactured medical test equipment that used disposable plastic test plates. These plates replaced the standard racks of test tubes. Being an innovation at the time, our throwaway test plates had become the cash cow of our laboratory equipment business.

Then we were challenged in an important market. The English National Public Hospital System had copied our plates and was manufacturing them itself. Even though the plates were patented in England, The National Public Hospital System manufactured the plates under the rationale of "compelling national interest."

We sued. The case went all the way to the Queen's Bench, the English high court. The court held surprisingly that the *patent* could be infringed in the national interest, but the *trademark* could not. What trademark?

Initially we did not see the trademark angle. It was our clever English barrister who spotted it. He found out that in molding our plastic plates our machinery made several round impressions. This was where push rods knocked the plates out of their mold. The English court determined, with our barrister's insistence, that the distinct size and location of our "knockout marks" were a distinctive design that was in fact a trademark. Because these "knockout marks" had been copied by the English hospital system's manufacturer, our trademark had been violated!

>>> *It does not cost much to develop good trademarks, and they can provide strong protection for your products and business. In addition, trademarks often lead to brand names and corporate identities. As your business becomes widely known in its markets, your brands will become assets of the highest value.*

A word of caution!

Patent and trademark attorneys will advise you never to use a trademark as a noun. Think about it. Once a trademark becomes a "generic," it is no longer enforceable. This happened to such good trademarks as "aspirin" and "escalator." It almost happened to Kleenex and Xerox. As the Xerox Corporation is fond of saying, to keep the distinction straight, "You can't xerox a Xerox. But we don't mind at all if you copy a copy on a Xerox® copier."

Copyrights

A copyright is an expression of an idea and not an idea or invention itself. Therefore, you would use a copyright to protect the text of your sales brochure or instruction manual. You can also use it for the article you write for a trade magazine, a script, or a software program. Your copyright should be identified by your name or company name, the © mark, and the year the copyright was made.

Copyrights are often a way to identify and legally stop people who are copying your business carte blanche. These commercial raptors do not stop with copying your product. They will often copy your brochures and instruction sheets as well. If you copyrighted your brochures and instruction documents and they violated your copyrights, you can stop them. It is often easier to demonstrate a copy of copyrighted material than it is to demonstrate the copy of a complex product. In any case, the copier's intention to steal your business is now firmly established.

Articles you write for trade magazines or newspapers often turn out to have considerable commercial value. Reproductions of these articles can be included with sales brochures to establish your reputation as an expert and leader in your field. Customarily, you assign the copyright to the publisher, but when you do, you should insist on the right to have reprints made for your own use.

If your business is based on artistic renditions, such as gift cards you design yourself, these should all be copyrighted. This is not an area to wait around and consider. If you have copyrightable materials do it now. Do not put it off.

Patents

All the aspiring entrepreneurs I talk to who are proposing a new product ask me about patents. "When the patent comes," they say in reverent tones, "big corporations will come running, eager to sign licensing deals and big royalties." The notion is that a patent will put the business on Easy Street.

It is heresy to say this, but frankly, patents are a mixed blessing. They are expensive, often costing over $8,000; they take several years to issue; they can inform your competitors about your special design; and they are not the final word. Patented inventions are often copied, and the validity of the patents can be challenged in court.

Before getting too far along, you should know that there are two main types of patents: utility patents and design patents. Both kinds can be applied to a product. You should also find a good patent attorney nearby and consult with him or her at the earliest stage in your invention process. You will find that the patent application and prosecution process gets very technical from the earliest stages and, if not done correctly, you may well lose your chance to receive an important patent.

Utility Patent

When we think of the traditional patent, we usually think of a novel design for, say, a better mousetrap. This is called a utility patent and must be novel, useful, and non-obvious to a person skilled in the technology. Furthermore, it is generally required that that the proposed design has been reduced to practice (in plain language, it really works). Usually the patent application text will include test data from your experiments that are convincing evidence that your design is indeed a better mousetrap.

Utility patents are more expensive than design patents and take longer to be approved—generally two to three years. They remain valid for twenty years from the filing date. You may do a Provisional Application. This gives you a year to file your patent application, but gives you the earlier filing date to establish the time of invention, in the event that the patent is eventually granted. During that year, the patent office does not examine your application for its merits.

The provisional application gives you protection for a limited time while you research your invention for marketability, talk to vendors, and discuss licensing. The application usually costs less than $1,000, patent attorney's fees included. If you find that the market is limited but an attractive niche, or crowded with similar inventions, then you should consider just blasting into the market without further pursuit of your patent application.

Design patent

Design patents are cheaper and easier to obtain than utility patents, and they often issue in one to two years. A design patent only covers the products appearance or ornamental aspects. Therefore, they are generally easy to design around by changing the product appearance. Design patents are valid for fifteen years from the date of issue. A design patent of the iPhone's appearance, not Apple's many utility patents for it, was key in Apple's legal attack preventing Samsung from copying its iPhone.

Therefore, if you have the resources, and appearance is important for your product in addition to its novel design, you should consider applying for a design patent as well as a utility patent.

Patent pending
Whether you have filed a provisional application or filed for a utility patent directly, or if you filed for a design patent, you can and should mark your product "Patent applied for" or "Patent pending." Most potential copiers of your product will forego copying your design until they see the patent when it issues. From then on, you must put your patent number on all applicable products, and you have to tell anyone who inquires what the patent number is. Then they can look up your patent application in a few minutes by an Internet search. In a sense, you had more protection during the time when your patent was applied for.

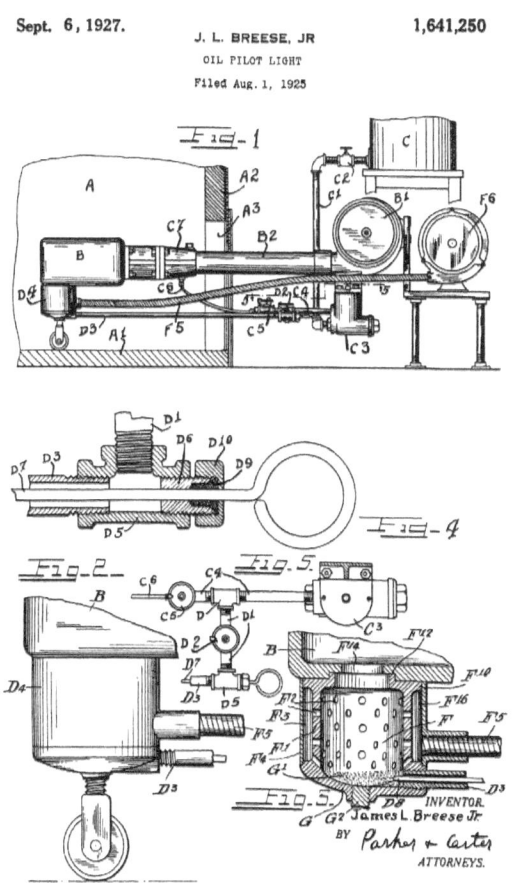

Sept. 6, 1927.

J. L. BREESE, JR

OIL PILOT LIGHT

Filed Aug. 1, 1925

1,641,250

Patent drawing from my grandfather James L. Breese's
oil burner pilot light patent, 1925. Simple ideas
evolve into complicated mechanisms.

Other Protection Strategies

For a small start-up company, producing a reliable product and developing a recognized brand name is often a stronger strategy than the shield of a patent. Think about it: what patents does McDonald's have? McDonald's has something better—it has a reputation for a reliable product and consistent service. IBM is a much higher tech company than McDonald's and has thousands of patents, but in the accounts of the Computer Wars, patents do not seem to have counted for much. Somebody else invented the personal computer. For Xerox, Polaroid, and some of the blockbuster drug companies, patents were important. Most of the time though, for small businesses, attention to product details and speed to the market are more important.

Again, I am reminded of the advice of a sage patent professor at MIT. Professor Rhines' counsel to our class of budding high-tech industrialists was: "Pot it, don't patent it." He was referring to electronic circuit design, and he meant protect the circuit from being copied by encapsulating it in plastic cement (called potting compound). If you break open the solidified plastic block a circuit is buried in to study the circuit, the circuit will be destroyed.

At my little company, Eco Sensors, we removed manufacturers' part numbers from key components in our products in order to slow down the copying process. Perhaps we could have found some patentable aspects of our circuits, but the time and cost involved to get strong patents did not seem worth the effort. If we could have found some patentable feature that would have multiplied our sales ten-fold, then of course we would suddenly get interested in patents.

Polaroid instant film is often cited as an example of what good patents can do for a clever inventor. But it is interesting to note that while Edwin Land, the inventor and the founder of Polaroid, was managing the company Polaroid relied on more than its patents to protect its position. Over the years, in my various high-tech industrial adventures, I did business with various Polaroid engineering and manufacturing groups. While they were proud of their patents, they were more concerned about protecting their secret know-how and identity of project objectives than any major company I have dealt with or heard about. They would never tell me how our products would be involved in their engineering or manufacturing, and projects often were identified only by code number.

Land started the business making experimental gun sights for the military in World War II and later non-glare sunglasses. Both products used properties of polarizing plastics that Polaroid manufactured. My father worked with Land on a gun sight project. It was only years later that Land invented instant photography film and developed the aura of a latter-day Edison. My father remembered him as an incurable optimist who was both patient and opportunistic.

Patent Fences

If you do receive a utility patent for an invention, it is often a good strategy to get more patents improving on the original filings that led to your first patent, These are thought of as an extension of the concept or yet another improvement of the art. These linked patents are often called a "patent fence," and, as the name implies, puts an ever more impenetrable barrier around your product. The additional patents are often easier to get than the first one because you and the patent office examiner develop familiarity with the product and its novelty.

The patent fence became the key part of Edwin Land's product protection strategy at Polaroid Corp.

After patenting a basic oil burner design, my grandfather would patent improvements to the design, and improvements to the improvements. My grandfather's design improvements tended to revolve around the electronic controls he developed for his oil burners. These controls provided the product advantage, which was the main value of the business in its final years. Over the twenty years that my grandfather developed oil burners, they were used in home furnaces, water heaters, as well as for commercial and military applications. In the 1930s through the 1950s, millions of these burners were sold, and my grandfather collected royalties from other companies who had agreements with him to manufacture and sell them. The income from royalties based on his patent fence gave him a good income for many years.

Patent Considerations for Small Businesses

For the most part, patents are most effective tools for large businesses. For pharmaceutical companies, the patent shield covers the huge cost of unique product development. A new cancer drug may take years and millions of dollars to develop. In addition, the large drug companies have the resources to defend the patent in a costly legal battle if it is disputed by another drug company.

On the other hand, for small businesses, what I have found is that patents can be worthwhile when:

- You are certain that you have a very large market. $100,000 of annual product sales probably is not worth patent protection. $10 million of annual sales probably is.

- Licensing of proprietary designs and know-how is a major part of the business. I was a director of a start-up company with novel technology to make safer automobile air bags. We were in no position to make the safety devices ourselves. We licensed major companies in Detroit to do it and pay us royalties. We would not dare go into the lions' dens at Ford or GM without strong patents.

- The small business needs to raise large amounts of venture capital. This is true because professional investors often like the reassuring protection of a patent. They may think they have found the next Xerox.

Our Family Experiences with Patents

Did patents help the bird feeder business?
My father received about a dozen patents for his bird feeders because of his creativity and early entry into the industry. Only a few of his patents were utility patents, which provide the most basic protection. Most were design patents, which are easier for competitors to design around.

What the patents did accomplish, however, was to allow him to collect royalties from infringers. The courts tend to be more sympathetic to your case if you do not try to prevent someone from infringing your patent, but instead settle upon a reasonable royalty settlement. But even my father said that, in retrospect, the cost of enforcing the patents and collecting the royalties probably exceeded the royalties received. On the other hand, the patents stoked his ego, and the patent numbers stamped on the bird feeders added a high-tech prestige element.

You never know who will try to infringe your patent
During the Second World War and the Korean War, my grandfather got government contracts for heaters to be used in barracks and tents. His friend, Jack Watson, an Army reserve colonel, later to become my grandfather's attorney, was called to active service in Korea. The North Koreans held most of Korea down to Pusan. He was there. Heating was poor, it was freezing cold, and facilities were rudimentary. Watson had to heat his washing and shaving water in his helmet on top of his old friend's *Breese Burners* space heater. But when Watson looked at the heater's label, he found that it was made in Japan!

The U.S. Army had contracted with a Japanese manufacturer to make the Breese Burners' heater design but had done nothing about seeing to it that appropriate royalties were paid to Breese Burners. Jack alerted my grandfather, who filed a claim against the Army in the U.S. Court of Claims. Luckily, an old college roommate of my grandfather's had gone on to become the Secretary of Commerce. After that, he became a partner in a powerful Washington, DC law firm. My grandfather enlisted his aid when he had to take on the U.S. Army. After protracted litigation, the court found in his favor, and the Army had to pay back royalties. Naturally, my grandfather felt vindicated by the decision, but the legal costs ate up most of his royalties.

A patent helped me raise venture capital
Flow Vision, my previous company, made instrumentation for the petrochemical industry. I started with one patent, which was immensely helpful in encouraging venture capitalists to

invest in the start-up company. Later I got more patents. I was never convinced, however, that any potential competitors were stopped dead in their tracks when they came across these patents. There might have been more aggressive competitors if there had been a bigger market for our products. In any case, we had secret know-how which was not revealed in the patents. This kept us three to five years ahead of anyone who might have tried to copy our products based on what they could glean from our published patent information.

Patents and proprietary information protection are a very emotional part of the business for the entrepreneur. To keep from losing perspective, you need a game plan for the business. You will be knocked about along the way, but the plan gives you perspective, gets you back on track, and shows how to actualize your vision for the future. In the next chapter, I will discuss how to make a business plan.

4

PLANNING YOUR BUSINESS

Sometimes, I think, the things we see
Are the shadows of things to be;
That what we plan we build...
Phoebe Cary, American poet

During the Bronze Age, sometime before recorded history, a lone figure started to trudge over the Alps from Northern Italy. After he left the mountain fields and had passed through the last forests before the barren summits, he apparently fell and died under a mass of snow. Discovered a few years ago by hikers, the Iceman, as he is now known, was found wearing relatively warm clothing and carrying a bow and arrows, a bronze hatchet and a pouch with medicinal plants.

Let's say that in his own small way the Iceman was a small businessman. Archeologists believe that he could have been fleeing attackers, looking for the last stray animals of his flock, or heading to Austria on a trading journey. I like to think he was heading north to trade. Before leaving his primitive mountain village, he might have said to himself,

"It's going to be a tough trip over the mountains. I will need arrows to kill five days worth of food; I will need a metal ax to cut firewood and help prepare the game I eat; I will need medicine; and fifty good sea shells to trade for bronze in Austria." If this was the Iceman's plan, it did not include a freak autumn storm.

Preliminary Planning

Since the Bronze Age, great civilizations have come and gone, but the essentials of business have not changed. A plan of some sort is essential, and it should answer the following questions:

What is my product or service?
What is my vision or concept for the business?
Do I have much competition?
What is the competition's pricing?
Do I have anything special that the competition does not offer?
What are my resources?
What are my goals?
How am I going to achieve my goals?
What additional resources are needed?
Where is my funding coming from?

No amount of planning could have saved the Iceman from the unexpected change of weather, but nowadays a good plan can avert many disasters.

Every business should have a plan. You need to know when and how much cash will be flowing in, and when and how much will be flowing out for supplies and other expenses. You should be able to postulate what the business looks like every year or so in its first few years. You must address each part of your plan even though many guesstimates are involved.

The Two Purposes of Any Plan

You will find that the plan serves two major purposes, and you may wind up with two versions of the plan to serve those purposes. One of those purposes is to help you think through your business in order to define it, staff it, finance, and manage it. The other major purpose is to help you raise investment capital.

Your plan eventually might be dozens of pages long with computer printouts of financial projections, photocopies of trade magazine articles, etc. This would be probable if you are planning to launch a high-tech product for great fame and fortune. On the other hand, if you are starting a modest business, your initial plan could be just a few pages. In either case, you should start with a single sheet of paper and summarize your plan's key points with handwritten notes. This early plan will be for your eyes only.

Let's say you are thinking of starting a business to design and sell electronic instruments to detect hazardous fumes in workshops. The plan is to make initial sales through a local distributor, later going national by finding larger distributors to cover the country, and then expanding the business worldwide through marketing via a Web site. To conserve capital, you will contract out your electronic manufacturing to specialty contract manufacturers.

Your preliminary plan notes might go something like this:

- Hazardous fumes detection - use Japanese sensor.
- Design and build electronics here.
- Many markets, such as woodworking shops, auto body shops, and dry cleaners.
- Follow the federal and local regulators for workplace safety.
- Start via local distribution and eventually go international via the Internet. Build a hazardous fumes and detection technology information database.
- Competitors – A, B, C . . .
- Our advantage is low cost and simplicity of operating our instruments.
- Sales - $100 thousand in first year or so to $5 million plus in 5 years.
- Preliminary cost analysis indicates I should break-even in three years.
- To start, we'll need a technician and an office manager. I'll do the product development and selling.
- We should be doing significant Internet sales within a year or we will be losing the opportunity.
- We will need: an office/shop/warehouse area ("flex space" at a business incubator?), electronics workshop, tools and equipment, a good computer, Web site, and starting capital.
- I (the founder) will manage. Key advisers will be local environmental and workplace safety experts, and electronics engineers. Need a good outside accountant.
- Capital sources:

Me - $50,000

Friends and relatives - $50,000

Local investors - $100,000 ("Doctors and lawyers")

Living expenses will be covered by my wife's salary
Bank loan against home equity and inventory - $50,000
Consider "crowdfunding" at an early stage.

As you decide what is important to you in your plan, you will find that most of the plan will be devoted to an area of particular interest or concern to your proposed business. You might want to focus on where your product advantage might be and how to divert attention from the entrenched competition. Are smaller instruments the key? Maybe the key is to design for longer battery life between charges. Maybe it is finding a new market niche that the competition has not even found yet. In my example above that would be something special for the fume-filled environment of automobile body shops.

You will have to do some field research to be sure your product concept and business strategy is a good one. Talk to a number of prospective customers in the various market niches you are thinking of targeting. People are usually flattered to have their opinions sought, especially if this is done by the inventor who is radiating entrepreneurial enthusiasm. You should also look for reports in trade magazines that pertain to your proposed business. Try talking to salespeople and distributors in your market area. Walk around a local trade show showing a prototype sample of your proposed product. The results of your research will be very helpful in strengthening your case when you begin raising investment capital.

Getting Professional Assistance

Seriously consider paying for outside assistance to fill in gaps in your plan. You can retain the services of an engineering design consultant, a patent specialist, a market research consultant, a specialty lawyer, etc., if that is what is required to get the business going.

The advantage gained from key professional assistance was pointed out to me in a trade magazine article. It was the story of a New England couple who were intrigued with the idea of starting a chain of coin-operated purified water vending machines. They planned to locate the machines in "refill center" kiosks. There is lots of water in New England, so they knew that selling the concept would be difficult. They spent about $6,000 on a marketing firm to have professional market research and analysis done. The firm studied the area, consumer profiles, and marketing approaches. The professional market researchers detailed where the couple should focus their sales efforts, how they should sell, and warned them about apparently promising areas which they should avoid.

Based on encouraging results and good strategy pointers from the study, the couple decided to start the business. The wife continued in her regular job while assuming the responsibilities of being the new company president. The husband found vending sites and serviced the vending machines. They gave away lots of free sample water. They went into debt but the article said that phase is mostly behind them. They are growing at a rate of about 40% a year.

When actually operating a business, it sometimes takes a while before you see where you need planning and operating assistance. My sister Anne, who is an artist and who now has a successful business in Maine merchandising her card designs, has been frustrated by the pros and cons of planning. She once wrote me, "My gut feeling was that there was a market for block printed cards of local light houses and ladybugs. I do wish in hindsight that I had had some real help in handling the money though. The amount isn't important. It's how it's handled and reinvested that counts." The years have passed and now she says her most important team members are a marketing partner who is organized and does her marketing planning and execution, and an accountant who keeps track of the money flows. With their support she is happy and creative, turning out ever more designs in her lucrative and satisfying business.

Raising capital

Since most entrepreneurs are looking for money when they are starting a business, let's look at the use of a business plan to raise capital.

The first thing you can do is to start calling and visiting local small business investment companies, venture capital firms and banks. To find good prospective investment companies, seek recommendations from your bank, your local small business incubators, the local office of the U.S. Small Business Administration, its business assistance arm, SCORE, and other similar sources. You must start somewhere and keep looking.

Venture Capital

Once you have an appointment to visit a venture capital firm, you suddenly can feel lonely and without resources. I have made many trips down this path and know the drill. You wait in a stuffy lobby a seemingly interminable amount of time. The minutes feel like hours when such a key appointment is in the offing. You are ushered into the smallish office of Dufus P. Huffnagle III. He is the junior partner. He is well dressed but fidgety and high-strung. He is looking at you like a lower being who is about to waste his valuable time. You look around and notice homemade reports piled everywhere: on his desk, in every corner of the office, on the spare chair, and in open boxes. That is when it dawns on you: your business plan is going to join that collection.

Indeed, he pops the question: "Say, did you bring a business plan we could review?" He will then ask a few short questions to get the gist of the business concept and to see what kind of material you are made of. Then he will glance at his watch and say something about "Running late, must catch the 4:02 now..." He does not want you hanging around, and he wants to keep you on the defensive. Your proposal has about one chance in ten of being pursued through more meetings and a one in a hundred chance of receiving investment from this firm.

Your chances are much better with a venture capital firm if you are introduced by a well-known businessman, lawyer, accountant or banker, or if your business is in a hot area like biomedicine or Internet technology.

Banks

Bankers, on the other hand, are a different breed of animal. They tend to be more easygoing and if they have any time available, they will listen to your pitch more patiently. Their approach is to save the crusher for last. "Aha! You don't have three years of profitable operation to show, you don't have an inventory of diamonds to collateralize, so let's see...what you can give us for security." (If this looks like a pawnshop approach, to some extent it is.) They tell you they will settle on real estate and securities. That means another mortgage on your home and signing over to their safekeeping those bonds your grandmother gave you.

Getting Results with Your Plan

I will talk about finance in more detail in chapter seven. However, I wanted to give you a sense of what may happen when you explore this area and how it may relate to your plan.

If you do not receive institutional financing but if your business does well, the business plan you left with these financial institutions can increasingly become your friend. When you return to seek capital again a year or so later, these investments executives will compare your actual results to your plan. If your results equal or exceed the plan they are going to get very interested. You will become a property worth betting on. If you have three good years in a row, both the venture capitalists and the bankers will be offering you financing you may not really want. "Them who has, gets…" etc.

A Sample Plan

If you are seriously looking for major investment money, such as from venture capitalists, banks, or project funds within an established corporation, then your potential investors will be looking for a more formal plan than will suffice for a start-up of a craft business. 30-50 pages along the following lines should serve:

- Summary
- Background
- Management. Summary of the key people and the roles they will play on this team.
- Description of the product or service. Make sure you describe your product or service in simple terms that the nonprofessional can understand with special emphasis on catering to a definite market need.

- Why this is a good time to introduce your product and why your company is the logical organization to do it.
- Proprietary considerations such as patents, copyrights, franchises, exclusive agreements, licenses.
- Market analysis, what you envision as your share of market, the competition, selling and pricing strategies, gross margin and revenue projections.
- Distribution methods and costs.
- Existing customers and sales. Size of orders, profitability, backlogs, references.
- Production facilities and methods. Competitive manufacturing cost analysis.
- Timetables and projected milestones.
- Risks and opportunities.
- Financial analyses. Usually several scenarios revolving around a base case. Capital requirements and share of ownership. Cash flow and cash position analyses derived from carrying forward projected balance sheets and income statements from one year to the next are the most scrutinized financial exhibits. These are usually done for several scenarios reflecting various sales, product development, financing and other assumptions.
- Organization plan and resumes of key personal with emphasis on relevant experience. Description of personnel duties and compensation plans. References.
- Bankers, lawyer, patent attorney, accountants and auditors, outside directors and other key advisors.
- Appendices, such as lengthy technical memoranda, supporting studies, trade magazine articles, summaries of relevant government policies and legislation.

After all this work (and believe me, many nights and week-ends will be devoted to producing the plan and its rewrites), you should try to figure out all the benefits you can derive from it. For example, your plan should force you to critically review your company's emerging strategy.

You should always be asking yourself, "What business am I really in?" When the Xerox Corp. first invented the plain paper copying process, they had the great insight that they were producing copiers to sell copying services. They were not in the copying machine business. The profit was in the service of copying and not in the copying machine itself. Therefore, they began their business by leasing the copying machines on a charge-per-page basis rather than selling the machines outright. The venture capitalists will often ask you in the first interview, "Are you selling the razor blades or the razors?" They are asking, "Is the money to be made in the equipment or in the supplies it consumes, and which part of the business are you going after?"

From the prospective investors' point of view, they are probably most interested in your future cash flow and cash position projections. These are the "bottom line" of new venture analysis, and they are a key method for determining the likely financing requirements. Usually the net cash position forecast for the next five years has a "J" or "hockey stick" shape. It is positive now and then in a year or so it goes negative, reaching the maximum negative point in two to three years. It is that maximum negative cash position that indicates the amount of outside financing required. As the product development matures and the market acceptance develops momentum, the cash flow goes positive and additional major outside financing may no longer be required.

My Plan to Raise Capital

My plan, which raised a million dollars for my polymer instrumentation venture, was relatively short. It was also mostly free of computer printout. We referred potential investors to satisfied customers. The new investors could visualize how they would profit from the momentum being established in a great new product. The timing was good—I was running out of savings.

The plan was twenty pages double-spaced. Most of the focus was on customer projects, analysis of the market, description of the personnel and their duties, and financial projections of the venture's profitability. The company, described in chapter one, had been operating for about two years primarily as a research project, with a few successful sales. In the plan, we clearly and convincingly described our market, our products, and our goals. Investors could see that the company represented a solid, well thought-out opportunity.

A New York venture capital firm committed for $500,000. When this psychological barrier was passed, it was relatively easy to raise $250,000 each from two other follower-type venture capital firms.

An outline of the plan, done in 1986, is:

FLOW VISION, INC.

Quality control instruments for the polymer and plastics industries

1 - SUMMARY DESCRIPTIONS

Background
When the company was founded and what it does.

Basic product line and its application.

Technical summary of the principles of the instrument's operation.

Why this instrument concept and design is needed now by customers.

Customers who are now using *Flow Vision* instruments.

Future product development projects and other growth strategies.

Markets

Identifies all existing customers, their applications of *Flow Vision* instruments, and the number of instruments each customer has. Customers include DuPont, Dow, Exxon, and General Electric. Estimated additional purchases by these customers. Short discussion of how the company anticipates developing future sales.

Sales

How sales have been generated. Discussion of selling by various means: in-house personnel, outside sales representatives, trade shows, and publicity releases in trade magazines.

Growth strategy

Identifies new product development projects, and indicates that acquiring other product lines or small companies may also be logical components of the growth strategy. Dollar expenditure estimates are discussed.

Manufacturing

States that it is best to have sub-assemblies done by outside contractors with final integration, testing, and shipping done in-house.

Venture capital requirements

Estimates that $1 million of venture capital is required. Important applications of the proceeds are product development, marketing, purchasing computer systems, opening a European office, hiring additional management, and building more inventory.

Sales scenarios

Two sales scenarios are summarized, starting with sales of $2 million or $3 million next year. Sales are estimated yearly for 5 years for the two scenarios reaching $10 million in the lower scenario and $20 million in the higher scenario. Cash balances are estimated each year for the high and low scenarios. Returns on investment are summarized in each case.

Personnel

One paragraph resumes of the six proposed key people: President, Vice President of Engineering, Vice President of Marketing, Controller, Director of Research and Project Engineer.

Listing of the proposed board of seven directors.

2 – EXHIBITS

Past financial performance

Sales, gross margins, and net incomes shown for the last two years. Sales started at $163 thousand and jumped to $474 thousand with the company almost breaking even.

Forward sales plan

Shows sales at $3 million next year increasing to $14 million in 4 years.

Product acceptability in various markets

Shows the advantages and disadvantages of *Flow Vision* instruments in such diverse markets as polymer production, pharmaceutical manufacturing, and marine biology research.

Sales potential by market

Shows potential *Flow Vision* sales in each of seven markets in four years.

Current financial statements

Shows the balance sheet and income statement for the fiscal year half-completed when this presentation was made. At this point, *Flow Vision* had almost no cash but was making a little money.

Application of venture funds

Shows how the estimated $1 million received in venture capital would be allocated among marketing, engineering, computers, Europe, inventory, general management, and moving to a new location.

Detailed breakdown of proposed engineering and market expenditures

Detailed cash flow projections for the next three years

For each year, there are starting cash positions, revenues, and detailed uses of the cash. The bottom line for each year is the cash balance at the end of the year.

Analysis of the expenditures directly related to receiving the venture funds

These include estimated legal fees, consulting fees, and repayment of some loans.

Detailed resumes of the key personnel

1-2 pages each.

Making a Plan for Your Own Use

Your business plan need not be only a tool to raise financing. Your plan can also help you manage your company. As a CEO, I have found the plan—particularly the part with the sales and cash flow forecasts—to be useful enough to occupy the strategic top-drawer position in my desk. You will find yourself constantly stealing a look at your plan to see how you are doing. I have found it helpful to keep a version of my plan in my computer as a series of spreadsheets. I update these as events happen, keeping my plan current and active. It also becomes surprisingly interesting and informative to review the statistics that accumulate from year to year. These could include your sales by product line, by key account, and by country, your monthly cash position, your quarterly profitability, etc.

The plan for my last company, Eco Sensors, Inc., needed only be for my own use because I did not need outside financing. Therefore it was more concise and without all the detailed explanations. However, should I have needed financing in the future, I would have all the background performance information ready for presentation.

As it happened, I sold my company in 2007, and my on-going plan was important for evaluating their prospective purchase by the buying company.

Every year I set sales and financial objectives for the coming year. I listed sales, gross profit, net income, products sold by category, and sales by market. There was also a page of text as a memorandum to myself describing new equipment and personnel needs, new products to develop, important trips or trade shows to schedule, key business goals to achieve, etc. At the end of the year, I wrote down the actual results and compared them to my goals. All this was inserted as a section in a three-ring binder that grew every year. The binder also included photos of new products and brochures, scenes on trips and at trade shows, snap shots of visitors and sales representatives, and other memorabilia. It is amazing how much better you feel about yourself, your employees and your business when you look through your plan and your company's history. Used in this way, your plan also gives you important insights for planning future developments.

To be useful, plans must produce positive outcomes. Therefore when you do your planning, avoid planning just for the sake of it. Do not let your plan development become an MBA thesis for members of your staff. Try to avoid the plan as an endless topic of staff meetings, which I have found is frequently the case with large companies. Set ambitious but realistic goals. Start writing and calculating and keep at it until you have a satisfying and useful guidance manual for yourself.

Periodic Reports to Investors

Your plan will serve as a good starting point for investor reports. Periodic reports are usually needed, and no matter how many investors you have or how formal or informal your relationship with them, an ongoing plan, where new information is presented as actual results, portrays a management that is goal-oriented and knowledgeable about where it is going. The report formats and other requirements requested by investors vary widely and are hard to generalize about, but as a rule, investors will want to have your balance sheet, income statement, sales and cash position forecast for the next quarter. They also like to see a page or so of commentary about current developments, future forecasts and upcoming expenditure requirements such as new personnel, equipment or major trips. They want to know, "Where are we now, where are we headed, what is the profitability trend, and what new developments will have to be dealt with."

Your Plan and Your Team

A one to three page summary of your plan is very useful for team building. I send a copy to all key employees for their information and comment near the end of the fiscal year. It definitely makes them feel more a part of the organization instead of just having a job, and they often contribute surprising ideas that I have not thought about. This summary plan can be a useful tool to show prospective senior level employees. It will stimulate their thoughts about the company. It will also give you feedback about how they might fit into your company. I have found that a simplified handout version of the plan can also be used to orient new employees. "Here's who we are, here's our vision, and here's where we are going." Wherever team building is involved, your summary business plan can become a very useful tool.

In the next chapter, I will discuss finding the people you need to make your winning team.

5

CREATING YOUR TEAM

I would rather invest in a grade A person and a grade B idea . . .
Folk saying among venture capitalists

It is not enough to have a great idea. Creating the new venture's team is vitally important. It takes about as much effort to define, find, and sign up a good starting team as it does to invent a new product. Looking back at the successes of many new enterprises I have managed, the selection of the initial key employees and advisors was usually the critical factor leading to the health of the companies. Looked at another way, success is more likely to come to the entrepreneur when he or she realizes that they cannot do everything themselves. Once having passed that hurdle, the entrepreneur then must purposefully seek out the very best people he or she can find for each job and avoid the temptation to hire friends, relatives, and cronies.

Investors and bankers generally look at the quality of the starting employee team before they scrutinize the quality of the product or business idea. The thinking seems to be that good people will recover after the failure of a poor idea and make the business a success anyway, but lesser quality people will mess up the exploitation of even a great idea.

Defining Your Role

Many successful small high-tech businesses are headed by a team of two senior people with complementary abilities (This same pattern emerges in many large corporations as well). The more extroverted or sales-oriented person is often known as "Mr. Outside," and the other more introverted person becomes the business manager, known as "Mr. Inside." The creative, technical, or engineering person can be either Mr. Outside or Mr. Inside, depending on his or her personality.

> >>> *It is crucial that the entrepreneur know whether he is a Mr. Outside or a Mr. Inside before proposing that another person be his partner in the team. He should also accept that neither job or role is more important than the other.*

In the beginning stages of the enterprise the relationship between the partners can be strained because of confusing identities. The creative engineer may prefer to stay in the lab, but customers may demand to meet the inventor, making the sales-oriented Mr. Outside feel as if he is being shuttled aside or put down. Mr. Inside may feel that salespeople are at best a necessary nuisance when Mr. Outside rides roughshod over fastidious accounting rules, such as providing the supporting documents for expense accounts.

Things even out when Mr. Outside and Mr. Inside appreciate their complementary abilities and work together as a team, recognizing each other's unique contributions. They may seem like the Odd Couple, but they are building a business. This approach is synergistic and could be thought of as $1 + 1 = 3$.

The Startup Company

To successfully launch the start-up company, you must begin assembling the best team you can find. First you have to determine how many and what kind of people you need. For instance, if you are going to start and remain a mom-and-pop operation, a non-degreed but proven and experienced accountant may be your best value. If you are starting as a corporation and have institutional venture capital investors, your Chief Financial Officer (CFO) should have a CPA.

The first few employees can make or break the success of your company. When one of those start-up employees turns out to be a miscast or a bad apple and you have to let him go, your emotional stress could be similar to shooting the family dog. He will invariably lay on the guilt trip about "being there from day one." Morally and emotionally, it is harder to terminate those who started with you on The Long March than to let go of the ones who joined the growing company later on.

Another problem that commonly arises with start-up employees is that they are often given titles that you later come to regret. The great salesperson, who helped start the company and to whom you gave only a modest salary but a big title such as "Vice President of Marketing," may not work out further down the road. If he does not have the wherewithal to be Vice President of Marketing as your company grows, it is going to be excruciatingly difficult to demote him and get him to work for a real Vice President of Marketing later.

Outside advisors and contractors must also be carefully selected. These include the company attorney, patent attorney, accountant, banker, advertising agency, a key distributor, consulting engineer, and board members. Usually one or two of these people turn out to be key for their timely and important advice at critical junctures. From my experience, I have never found it worthwhile to seek bargains when selecting these advisors. The cheapest attorney may be worse than no attorney at all. Your friend who does personal tax returns may be way out of his depth on your corporate work. The distributor who will sell for a lower discount may not sell much. At the startup stage you need all the help you can get, but the place to cut costs is not on advisors and professional assistance.

Starting Small

Your core group of employees will be more interested in their work and more loyal to the company if they are kept busy pursuing a common goal. They should not be distracted by the thought that a too large payroll is stretching you too thin and jeopardizing their future with your company. For this reason, I have always found it best to start the company with a minimum number of employees. Specialists and helpers for overload situations can be contracted as needed.

Try not to set up a huge payroll at the beginning. The cash drain can be frightening; the effects on overall employee morale bad; and the employees can be difficult to terminate. The initial employees do not need to be hired full-time. They could begin as moonlighters, part-timers, consultants, or as advisors. The benefits work both ways. You are looking them over and seeing where they fit in, while they are looking at you and your business to see if it is worthwhile to jump ship from a good job somewhere else to join you.

>>> *Avoid hiring friends and relatives who will work for lower pay and whom you think will be more trustworthy and loyal. (Often the opposite turns out to be the case). Also, avoid hiring people to whom you owe a favor. Pay them back some other way.*

Be wary of people recommended by outside investors to "round out the team." You may find that you have more employees than you need and a suffocating payroll as a result. At my polymer instrumentation company, *Flow Vision*, the investors thought we should have a clearly identified Vice President of Operations, a Vice President of Engineering, and a Vice President of Marketing. At the time, all of these functions were covered by existing personnel doing more than one job. By filling in all the positions on the standard organization chart and catering to the investors' sense of security, our operating costs increased several hundred thousand dollars per year. Therefore, when the recession hit a few years later, we no longer had the cash reserves to tide us through the economic downturn. We were forced to sell the company.

In summary, here are some key points to keep in mind when thinking about putting together your team:

- Focus on what jobs are lasting and really need to be done. Hire for these jobs only. Avoid excessive employment commitments by using contractors, consultants, and even software packages.
- Hire friends and relatives only as a last resort. Keep the atmosphere professional with people hired based on skills, experience, and attitude.

- Look for employees who will help you to bridge your next stage of corporate growth. Hire people who know how to network or who already have networks of their own established with people in your industry.
- Keep the company personnel focused on common corporate goals. For example, if you think that a key goal is to develop a particular new product, let everyone know it. That way, your staff will be able to interpret your reactions better and to better supportive your efforts.

Finding People

Finding the right people for your company when you need them can seem like a daunting task. You start out full of hope, thinking that just about anyone who captures your interest would be delighted to join your team. Then you find that quite a few likely candidates do not share your vision, or do not want to commute to your location, or just cannot cut the cord with their present employer. The reality is that you will have to cast a wide net, catch many fish, and throw most of them back.

I have no magic formula for the problems of recruiting except to advise you to search for team members using as many sources as possible. Do not be constrained to one personnel agency. Do not just put an ad in the paper. Try everything! Look for people through all of the following ways and more, if you can think of them:

- Newspaper ads. I have done better with this medium than any other for all levels of employment.

- Internet sources including LinkedIn.com for senior employees and Craigslist.com for local, lower level employees.
- Personnel agencies. Get one where a senior recruiter really understands your needs. This approach can work well. Agency fees however, can be up to 1/3 of a year's pay or more. That can be very tough on a start-up company.
- Temporary help agencies. Hire one of their people for a while. If things are going well, hire him or her permanently. This approach is often less costly than personnel agencies and gives you a chance to test potential employees.
- State and other government employment departments. I have never had any luck here, but you might do better.
- Job postings on the bulletin boards of trade schools, colleges, and universities. This approach has worked moderately well for me. You do not need to make the trip to the institution yourself. Call the department secretary, and he or she will post your job description. These facilities really want to place their graduates and you just might get lucky and find a go-getter who is ready to learn. You might also find a summer student, co-op student (work and study), research intern, etc.
- Friends. Ask them if they know of someone who fits your requirements.
- Networking in the industry. Go to trade meetings, industry receptions, and the like to network for employees.
- Trade shows. The classical bazaar for swapping resumes.
- Salespeople who call on you and other companies are often very tuned in about who is approachable for job openings.

The Interview and Resumes

Be sure you have the job descriptions written down for reference during employment interviews. Have a firm figure in your mind about the pay and other compensations for each job. Interviews go much better when it is apparent that you know what you want and how much it will cost. The interview time should be spent focusing on other areas, such as the candidate and the company.

Every job candidate will produce a resume. The problem is that it is very difficult to get in-depth background information about any employment candidate. Letters of recommendation have all but disappeared from the business world because of fears of legal repercussions if the statements are in any way defamatory. Personnel departments simply give the employee's name, position, and service dates. The candidates' resumes all tend to look like you are interviewing a one-in-a-million find of the century. Typical excerpts are:

Raised sales over 25% a year.
Organized engineering department in two months.
Fluent in Russian, Greek, Portuguese and 3 other languages.

It would be much easier and fairer to all concerned if someone could write a letter highlighting who the prospective employee really is. My father once wrote an open letter to a would-be employer about me, which began:

I sometimes wish that people would be supplied with a card of information such as is provided with oil burners and other mechanical equipment. As I look at the card describing my oil burner, it lists the dos and don'ts, as well as the name of the serviceman to call and simple remedial measures that can be taken to correct faults. I trust the following letter will take the place of such a set of directions.

Written over 50 years ago, his description of me is still right on target:

Lawrence (as he called me) *is basically a theoretical person, more interested in abstract ideas than in the execution of them. If he carries an idea to completion in material form, it is more the embodiment of an idea than a mechanical marvel. In carrying out an idea he does it in the most economical form and in the shortest time possible.*

When Lawrence becomes interested in a new theory in electronics, he will work far into the night and all day in order to complete it. He will do this work in the shortest possible time, taking many short cuts which shows a very inventive mind.

Lawrence is almost useless on work which is of no interest to him. If given a straight job of work, such as polishing or painting, which does not occupy his mind, his thoughts will travel. His finished work is seldom a pleasure to look upon. If he is required to do a good complete job, he will do so, but continual urging is necessary.

I believe Lawrence will be extremely valuable to the person who can realize what his abilities are and who has the problems to solve to which Lawrence can be applied.

Sincerely yours,
Peter Kilham, President
Curvit Corporation

The next best thing to such a letter is to employ a person on a trial basis. After a few months, the real personality emerges. This is especially important in a start-up company where one bad apple can quickly spoil the barrel. The most practical way to do this is to start the prospective employee out as a contract employee or as a contractor until you are satisfied that they will work out as a regular payroll employee. This approach can produce unexpected positive benefits. Perhaps the person was taken on as an engineer and you discover after a week or so that he or she is actually a born salesperson. Then when you make a permanent offer to this prospective employee, you can propose the best job definition for all concerned.

Employees for the Wrong Reasons

Hiring people because they stroke your ego is a dangerous and expensive move. Cliques of under-worked employees, who cater to their boss's ego, tend not to be supportive when trouble develops. I have often seen these people hired under the guise of being "good advisors." This happened to my grandfather. Although he had a very successful oil burner development business, he had surrounded himself with a clique of "yes men" consisting of a senior engineer, an attorney and an accountant. When the time came for him to attack the U.S. Government in court for not paying him royalties on the use of his patents, these senior courtiers balked at testifying. They demanded fat fees beyond their regular salaries for their testimonies. My grandfather could have had better advisors at a lower cost if these people had not been on salary. He should have paid them only for their professional time actually used on his behalf and foregone the expensive pleasures of a small court with himself as the king.

Yourself as the Leader

There is one member of your team we have not talked about yet and that is you. It is crucial that you be realistic about yourself. Other members of the team will come and go, but we will presume that you are at the helm. Or should we? Maybe your product idea and vision will make a great company, but are you better suited to be the head of research or chief sales person rather than chief executive officer? You may find this an ego-bruising decision, but assuring survival and growth of the enterprise is normally what is important. Ask yourself some searching questions about yourself:

- **Why are you creating this leadership job for yourself?** Is it to escape from some other job working for someone else? Are you a visionary leader? Do you have the resources available to get started? Do you have experience in this line of business? In other words, are you starting this new company with yourself at the helm because it is a sound business idea and you are the one to do it? Or are you indulging in a form of escapism, pursuing a romantic notion of being in business for yourself? Try to be honest with yourself about your motives. Remember, true leaders never tire of leading the charge even if they stop a few arrows along the way.
- **Are you trying to make a business out of your hobby?** Be careful that you are not expanding what has been a satisfying hobby into what is going to be an unprofitable

pursuit. Tying fishing flies is very satisfying but probably no lone individual can make a good living from it any more. In addition, the business day for the typical entrepreneur allows little time to pursue his or her hobby—be it jewelry making or electronics. Most of the day will be spent guiding employees, seeing customers, negotiating the rent, waiting to see someone at the bank, anything but enjoying the pursuit you used to love as a hobby. As I have mentioned before, the IRS looks very carefully at hobbyists posing as business people. They know that most hobbies are not profitable. Consequently, The Agency tends to take the position that deducting hobby expenses as business expenses is unacceptable. As far as they are concerned, there is not a serious business unless you can show an ability to make a consistent living from it. The best hobby is one which gives you enjoyment without thinking about it every day.

- **Are you willing to cut your income by a large amount for several years?** (including health insurance and retirement plan). Every once in a while a proven entrepreneur, with a billion dollar idea, leaves the big corporation and manages to convince his investors that he should be paid $250,000 a year salary plus bonus, stock options, and expensive car from day one. In real life, these cases are few and far between. For every one of these instant success stories, there are 10,000 more cases of entrepreneurs starting up with no pay except the husband's or wife's income, perhaps some consulting fees, maybe something wangled from the unemployment office, and even a raid on the kids' college fund. It is an adventure-a-minute for the first few months, and then grim reality (mortgage payments, children's college tuition) sets in. Also, even sure-thing financing has a way of appearing months after the promised date. Great financial sacrifice is done because you believe passionately in your new idea.

- **Are you willing to do whatever it takes?** This is kind of an open-ended question, but what I mean is: can you put up with licking stamps, standing in line at the UPS counter, buying office supplies, and doing the windows now that you are no longer a VP of Marketing with five assistants? You used to be able to get another phone line or computer by calling Central Services. Back then some lower caste member would bow and scrape and come up with the delivery. Then the phone company says the lines are hard to get right away and, incidentally, they would like a deposit. So, for a while, you will have to share a phone line with your teenage daughter or do everything with your smartphone! By definition, an entrepreneur must have a can-do mentality.

- **What does your family think about all this?** Most family members in their heart of hearts will recoil in horror at the thought of mom or dad leaving their lifetime job (however dull and modestly paying) at the local bank to start a new company. Impoverished relatives come out of the woodwork, however, when word is out that the long struggling visionary died with millions stashed away. When my father, who built up a multimillion-dollar business, passed away, family and friends gathered around the lawyer for the reading of the will. He left his business to the employees! He never felt that his family was solidly behind him from day one, so why should he give them the business now? Families are usually ambivalent about the Patriarch's new venture, and he or she must rationalize their lack of full understanding.

- **How do you deal with failure?** Do you see failure as the end of life as you know it? Or do you see it as a temporary setback in life's great adventure? To the pessimist, every day of a new business will produce a negative incident showing the folly of it all. The optimist will stubbornly chip away at every problem—business or technical—until fate gives up and success is assured. A common trait for my grandfather, my father, and me was that we all had business setbacks and failures, but each of us regrouped and created a success the next time around. To the real entrepreneur a failure is merely a setback in the greater path of success.

- **How about your basic leadership skills?** Do people naturally listen when you talk? Are you enthusiastic even when facing adversity? Do you always find the path when the others have lost the way? Entrepreneurs who are successful company-builders tend to have strong self-esteem, are goal setters, pay attention to details, and have life and communication skills.

Being successful as an entrepreneur means knowing who you are and what you are actually capable of in the real world. A small at-home business does not mean you can hide out. Your contacts as a businessperson mean others will depend on you for your decisions and know-how. You have to be willing to shoulder that responsibility.

If you are willing to take control and guide your business, and if you and your family are willing to risk the house, the car, and your hidden funds to pursue your dream, then you are a good candidate for successful entrepreneurship. If you then surround yourself with good people for the right reasons, you are likely to be a success at your new business.

Now that you are the great leader with a great team, there is no time to lose. The pressure is on to sell something. We will get into this in the next chapter.

6

MARKETING AND DISTRIBUTING YOUR PRODUCTS

Customers don't buy *products. They buy satisfaction.*
Old business saying

It has taken me many years to learn that customers buy satisfaction and not products. If customers buy more and different products from you, it is because they were satisfied with the products they purchased earlier. If they buy your products through a distributor, it is in part because that distributor has created a reputation for customer satisfaction. Marketing is the process of finding, communicating with, and selling to those customers who will be satisfied with your products. Marketing is usually the most expensive operation of a company and often the most difficult to measure quantitatively the outcomes of efforts. For example, it is often observed that, "Half of advertising works, but you never know which half." Therefore, planning your marketing carefully is an absolute must for a successful company

Pitfalls to be Avoided

Because many promising technically based businesses founder because of misdirected marketing, I think some words of caution are in order. These are some of the business mottoes I have run across which constitute pitfalls in the area of marketing:

1 - "*A great product sells itself.*"
Whether the product is a piece of beautifully crafted handiwork or a spin-off of the latest space technology, people can be fascinated by a product and still not buy it. Interest in a product is not necessarily a strong intention to purchase. Many technical and inventive entrepreneurs mistake the polite admiration that people show for their products to be valid market research and strong buying interest. Nevertheless, after the satisfying experience of having friends say that you have a marvelous invention, you should back up and ask yourself:

a) Is this a product that is really needed?
b) Is it priced competitively?
c) Is it packaged attractively?
d) How will prospective buyers find out that the product exists?
e) Where will they buy the product?

All these questions need answers when you are considering a marketing direction and strategies for reaching and selling to the public.

2 - *"Good marketing and advertising can overcome product deficiencies."*
High-tech start-up companies, and others under intense sales pressure, very often feel that known imperfections in product design can be overcome by selling harder. "Just get the customers to buy it, and they will love it." These defective or poorly engineered products may be returned for refunds, but the negative image of your company can spread through the entire trade. This can be devastating for a new company. Think of the Chevrolet Corvair. It is a classic example of an innovative product that irretrievably sank under the weight of a poor reputation. It became the often-cited example of American automobile industry engineering and manufacturing decline that helped open the doors to an onslaught of imports.

3 - *"Tiny firms can sell big systems."*
New companies are starting up each day attempting to engineer, manufacture, sell and service something akin to a Boeing 747s. My father and I both got smart relatively late in life. We both had owned companies making large, complex products that generated suffocating marketing and service costs. Then we both changed our tactics. My father's bird feeders and my gas sensing instruments are both examples of products which are easily manufactured by a small business. They fit in smallish boxes and can be shipped quickly and inexpensively. Customers can easily learn how to use them. They can be purchased by credit card, and unlike our previous big system products, our marketing does not have to include long customer approval trials, expensive installations,

or extensive after-sale customer support. We are not immune from competition, but even if a new competitor turns out to be IBM, we have a good chance of dealing with them.

4 - *"Engineering projects are products."*
Selling highly engineered but incomplete products in the name of being a product business is a common start-up problem of technology businesses. Each "product" is rationalized as the salable result of an interesting project. Selling these custom-engineered products usually does not lend itself to volume marketing methods. Selling is typically achieved by the charm and persistence of the inventor. Traveling and constant presentations become tiresome and expensive, and the market can be quickly saturated. Once the founders are exhausted, the realization dawns that they should have developed at least one standard product that many people would love to have. Engineering projects-as-products develop for any of several reasons. One is the lack of interest by many techno-entrepreneurs in production and marketing. They think if an engineer can build it and a friend wants it, "We are on our way!" Another reason is the lack of persistence about product commercialization. "We'll make a few special widgets and see how they go, and then we'll improve a little." Meanwhile it becomes difficult to break out of the perpetual development mode. A few salespeople keep things going, but competitors can have discovered the basic product idea and begin setting up efficient production and marketing to build real businesses. Many of the early laser and computer companies started this way and sank without a trace.

To avoid these pitfalls, you must have a product that not only fits the capabilities of your company and market, but one which has been sufficiently perfected so that there is general customer satisfaction. When that aspect is well underway, you should go about marketing with the same thoroughness that you might use designing a new product. To one degree or another, you have to be prepared to address market research, sales methods, distribution, advertising, branding, and the Web in order to get your product into the marketplace.

Researching Your Market

Market research has two general uses:

1) It gives you important information for your own use in selling your product. It should give you vital information about your target markets and what market applications will be most productive for you. Besides the "who" will buy, your market research should tell you "why" and "how" they will buy. In addition, you will learn your market-acceptable price points.
2) The research will become a very important part of your corporate plan, especially if you ever expect to be taken seriously by professional investors.

You will need to develop background information and a strategic vision of why a company like yours has an opportunity at this moment in time. Here are some of the questions you will want your market research to answer:

- Who are my real customers that will become my core markets?

- What product design or service package is acceptable to a large number of customers?
- How many of my products can I sell per year?
- Who is the competition and about how many comparable products are they selling?
- How is marketing and distribution generally done in my industry?
- Is my strategy to have a different or better product (such as a 100-mpg car)? Or is my strategy a different distribution approach (such as Dell selling its own computers via the Web)?
- Should my marketing and sales personnel be in-house staff, or should they be talent contracted through ad agencies, distributors, and other marketing firms?

There must be flexibility in your thinking (and in the thinking of your investors and directors) of course because market research is still an inexact science. I started an instrument design with outdoor pollution measurement in mind; its first market turned out to be hospital sterilization rooms; and it wound up in indoor ozone measurement! Nevertheless, any significant market research gives you a product design and marketing starting point, and your evolving market model will be the core of your general corporate plan as the years go by.

Gathering Marketing Information

Market research information has to be pieced together wherever you can find it. Helpful information about market size, sales trends, and changing interests in products and services often can be found in many places without great cost to your new company. Valuable information can be gathered from trade publications, through trade shows, from government agencies, and increasingly on the Web.

I learn a lot by just getting out and talking to as many people in the business as possible. I talk to top executives as well as people selling on the street. Here are some important information sources:

Trade shows

Trade shows are one of the best places to run into many informed people. Once you wade into a trade show, put shyness aside and talk to people. You will find many who are informed enough to offer helpful comments about your new product and venture.

Professional societies

Meetings of the local chapters of professional societies are often excellent places to mine for information. Some industries have local networking get-togethers on a regular basis. These are usually social situations such as cocktail hours. Find out about these gatherings Web research, the headquarters of the trade group, and announcements in the trade media.

Networking

Network as much as possible. I find I can get a mixture of market size information, comments on product concepts, leads on potential employees, and trade contacts with this approach.

>>> *Always have plenty of business cards with you. Make sure these are quality printed and with some color in addition to black and white. Hand out an extra card if it is likely to be passed onto a valuable contact or potential customer sometime*

in the future. Always have some brochures that are folded to fit an inner jacket pocket. These can be discretely handed out as the occasion demands.

Show a Prototype of Your Product

I suggest always creating a sample product. Make up one or two prototypes and some provisional data sheets. With these in hand, visit as many prospective customers as you can. If you plan to use distributors, show them the prototypes also. Take them to trade shows. Have a prototype in your car when you go to professional society meetings or gatherings. A model is worth a thousand pictures! Nothing will elicit both product development and market research information like showing prototypes of your proposed product to prospective customers.

Marketing consultants

Marketing consultants can be expensive for a start-up business, but they can be worth it if they are very experienced in your particular market. If you decide to hire a marketing consultant, be sure their assignment is tightly focused. For example, if your product is a radon detector for the home market, have your marketing consultant focus on "radon detectors for the home" and not simply "radon detectors" or "home sensor systems." The tighter the focus and the more specific to your product, the more valuable the information will be for your company.

Published information and interviews

The best market research usually combines a comparison of published information with interviews with typical prospective customers. In our example, trade magazines indicate that there is a potential annual U.S. market for one million home radon detectors. In interviewing heads of household in your area and showing them your prototype radon detector, you calculate that 1 in 10 would buy your device. That is a lot more than one million annually in the U.S. Why the difference? Is your area not typical? Are the trade magazine estimates factoring in inefficiencies in advertising and distribution which you did not account for? Resolving these market research discrepancies will help you think through a better marketing strategy.

>>> *Incidentally, I have found that market research usually overestimates annual sales for a relatively unknown product by a factor of at least 10. Salespeople usually overestimate their next year's sales by a factor of at least two. When I do my market research and have asked for sales estimates, I then deflate the figures I get from sales people by these rules-of-thumb. Then everything comes out more or less to prediction!*

Many companies get market research consulting by starting out a prospective *Vice President of Marketing* as a *Marketing Consultant.* If the results are good, then they may be considered a prime candidate for the job of *Vice President of Marketing.* It is important to remember that the v*ice president of marketing* usually has responsibility for sales as well. In a small company, the salespeople will report to him or her. In larger companies, the sales manager usually reports to the vice president of marketing .

What you need to consider when using this method of selecting a VP of marketing is that managing a sales force is quite different from effective marketing research and consulting. The potential marketing executive will have to be thoroughly reviewed before a final decision is made to have this person handle both slots.

I recall that when I was a salesperson for a biomedical equipment company, we had a vice president of marketing who did not have a clue how salespeople worked and a sales manager reporting to him who did not have a clue where the market was going. For the few years I was there, these two champions of their own causes floundered because they could not put together mutually supportive policies.

How to Price Your Products

A good rule of thumb for product pricing is that the product's "list" (published) price should be *at least* four times its manufactured cost. This should include parts, labor, and overhead. Many entrepreneurs as well as apparently sophisticated businessmen have a hard time swallowing this reality. However, in my experience here is what happens: marketing costs and distributor discounts take at least 50% right off the top. Now your cost is about half of what you receive after marketing and distribution are factored out. From that figure subtract out administration, engineering, and various operating costs and you might have 10-20% of sales left over as a pre-tax profit. From that, your business must make a return attractive to investors and still have enough earnings to reinvest in growth.

Pricing is closely involved with marketing because marketing can often be the single biggest cost for many new companies. When you are pricing your product, make sure the price honestly includes your marketing costs. Many new entrepreneurs make the mistake of under-pricing. They are afraid customers will be scared off by apparently high prices. While this may be true at Wal-Mart, it is rarely a prime consideration at a start-up company with an important new product. Although customer feedback is important for deter-mining pricing, remember, *customers buy satisfaction and that includes many things besides price. You must more than cover your costs. Remember that it is a lot easier to lower prices, if required, than to raise them.*

Choosing the Best Sales Methods for Your Products

After determining marketing strategy, finding the right sales method will be one of the most crucial decisions a new busi-ness will make. Choosing the right one or ones will be one of your most important decisions.

Some of the sales methods are (these will be described in detail below):

- Direct salespeople.
- Distributors who buy and resell.
- Representatives, who sell your products to distributors or your ultimate customers for a commission.
- A toll-free phone number listed in your advertisements.
- Yellow Pages advertisements.
- Direct mail solicitations.
- Telemarketing.
- Direct selling via a "store" on the Web.

Any combination of these techniques could work for your new company. Good marketing involves quickly finding out which of these techniques will be the most productive for your products. The results are often not intuitively obvious. Let's explore the most important sales methods to see what might be best for you.

Your own sales people

It is human nature to want full control of the sales effort and to want to save money by not giving a cut to a middleman. That is why many start-up companies will start out with their own sales people. The idea is that they will work for a sales commission. That way there is no cash drain until sales are made.

The classic problems that can creep in when using your own in-house salespeople are these: (a) The salespeople will begin to demand an advance or "draw" against future commissions. (b) They will run up high travel and entertainment expenses. (c) In lieu of that, they will agitate for a company car. (d) A sales manager will be hired to manage the salespeople, but proven sales managers do not come cheap. They can demand a stellar salary plus an incentive based on sales. He or she may want a better car than the sales people and regular sales meetings in expensive resorts.

I once had a company where we manufactured complex instruments to monitor the quality of chemical production. Our customers were large chemical plants, which are traditionally located in remote areas. We had to make sales and service visits to these plants ourselves because in most countries, including the United States, we could not find suitable distributors. These trips were very expensive. Marketing and sales expense, which was originally budgeted at 10% of sales, grew to 35% of sales. Our profit margins were wiped out. Manufacturer's agents, with their commissions, began to look better and better.

Distributors

A typical distributor will look for 25%-50% discount from your listed sales price. While at first this may seem like a lot to give up, consider the following pluses:

- They usually have professionally produced catalogs and Web sites.
- They have efficient distribution and warehouse facilities.
- They will most likely distribute other manufacturers' products which may be much better known than yours. Your products can benefit from the loyal following developed for that distributor's sales of better-known products.
- The distributor's reputation can open doors your unknown name in selling your product.
- Distributors who buy and resell products are under self-imposed pressure to sell everything they purchase.

On the other hand, distributors often are not effective for very complex products that involve a lot of factory training for their sales people. They tend to prefer products which can be learned by studying a few brochures and technical papers.

Sales representatives
Another approach to selling your new product is to use sales representatives. These are independent sales people who sell a group of compatible but not competing product lines. They will usually work for a straight commission. Their commission is often less than a distributor's discount. This apparently lower cost seems attractive, and it may work well if the representative knows your products very well and if personal sales contact is important in selling your products. Representatives are well suited for selling complex technical products where they have a long relationship with the factory and have had in-depth training.

Remember that representatives, as opposed to distributors, usually do not have an investment in your inventory because they did not buy your product to resell. Therefore, they may not try as hard to sell the product as a distributor would who is trying to "turn" his inventory.

>>> *Be wary of the representative who has taken on your products mainly to show customers he represents products for every application. It is likely that your products will not be featured in his presentations but will become afterthoughts to discuss if the time is available.*

Toll-free phone number

The "800" number (footnote: they have run out of 800 numbers so, as of this writing, they are offering 888, etc.) is a very effective sales tool for many companies including technology-based ventures. A burden in selling high-tech products has always been educating prospective customers about the technology involved, the engineering features of the product, and the consequent advantages for the customer. In the past, this education was done by factory "sales engineers" or trained independent "factory reps."

Supporting such traveling specialists is now so expensive that in many cases it is cheaper to give the customer a toll-free number to call a factory expert direct. If the customer is given good information and advice by a factory engineer, the confidence engendered often makes the sale happen without a salesperson involved. Overseas customers could not call us via the 800 number so they achieve much the same purpose by "dialoguing" via e-mail. Five or six e-mails may bounce back and forth before the sale is made. In my previous company, Flow Vision, we were maintaining a force of traveling sales engineers, and the cost nearly killed us. In Eco Sensors, we publicized our 800 number and e-mail address, and sales have been brisk at a low per sale cost.

Yellow Pages advertising

The *Yellow Pages* was one of the great ideas of Bell Telephone, the father of all our phone companies. Everywhere I go in the world, I find that the local phone directories have their yellow pages section. Many businesspeople I talk to find that *Yellow Pages* advertising is their principal marketing tool. It can work well if your business caters to a local area about the size of a county.

My businesses sold all over the world and so the *Yellow Pages* did not help us. Web-based information search services are probably going to predominate for the global information search.

Direct mail and email solicitations

Sooner or later almost every new business tries sending out brochures with persuasive cover letters to thousands of "hot prospect" customers. It was very popular in the 1950s through the 1980s. The advent of wide-scale usage of 800 numbers and Web-based marketing has cooled this approach, at least for technology-based products. To be effective and avoid the junk mail look, extra costs are recommended to catch the recipient's attention such as first-class stamps and quality color brochures.

Recipients' answer rates tend to be, at most, a few percent. Answering the returns is labor-intensive and costly. The method may still be effective for a very highly focused mailing list, such as participants to a technical conference in your industry.

A more current method is email letters to your list with technical information attached and a link to your website. A problem with this approach is that your emails can be blocked as spam. To avoid this, you should have a person's name in the address line, do not use words like "special deal," "great savings," "free trip to Cancun," etc., and be sure there is a standard unsubscribe or "opt out" box at the end of your message. You can use emailing apps like mailchimp.com, which will give you a very professional and efficient mailing. They will require that all your addressees approved having your email solicitations sent to them

Telemarketing

Telemarketing has a bad image. Everyone knows about the high-pressure sales pitches that come at dinnertime for everything from long distance telephone service to charities. I am not aware of this method working well for selling complex products. However, I have seen it used effectively by industrial companies who are following up on leads they developed at trade shows.

Direct selling via a "store" on the Web

Much has been said about Web-based selling by Web-based retailers such as Amazon.com of such consumer items as books and music. Almost overnight, the stock market has accorded them higher value than the old-line retailers and department stores. This is truly a commercial revolution in the traditional way of retailing to the public. The Web has also proven to be equally effective, if not perhaps even more so, for small businesses in selling specialty products, high-tech products, and business-to-business services. The small high-tech company can explain its products and applications in great detail through an extensive Web site avoiding much of the cost of employing technical sales people. The other point about Web-based selling to bear in mind is that the growing number of ever more sophisticated search engines makes finding your site easier by the use of the purposeful searchers who are your prospective customers.

Most of my company's sales have been through distributors, and so our Web site has been in large part to support my distributors. They all have had excellent Web sites. Because Internet is so important, marketing via the Web will be discussed in detail in the next chapter, which is solely addressed to how to use its potential for your new business.

Advertising

Advertising needs to be part of your total sales strategy. Even when you are using distributors or sales representatives to do all of your selling, advertising will help them by creating customer awareness of your products and their benefits. But where to advertise? Advertising agencies are fond of saying, "Half of your advertising works great, but you never know which half." My experience has been that you do not need to give up that easily. With a little concentrated effort, you can narrow down the list of publications and other media where advertising really works for you. *The key in your media selection process is to ask the customers who call for more information about how they found out about your products.* Find out if it was from an advertisement and if so, in which publication. Before very long you will know what ads are working for you.

I have found that for small start-up companies, advertising is usually lost in the slick trade magazines. These trade magazines that initially look so appealing can lose a small new product in their crowded glossy formats. Your potential customers may skip over your little ad while admiring the big ones from the mega-companies with the glossy full color photos. These companies have seemingly unlimited advertising budgets. I have found that ads appearing in the smaller publications which cost far less and are geared to appeal to focused interests are often more productive. When considering advertising, do not overlook regional newsletters and professional society journals. They offer a more level playing field between big and small companies. Their readership is highly focused, and their advertising rates are often much less than the high gloss trade magazines

Direct sales media

For selling by direct mail, phone calls (telemarketing), or emails, it is easy to do limited trials with lists of 25-100 names. If more than 5% of the customers contacted in this way respond with at least requests for more information, you have found a responsive sales approach. The key to success and well-spent advertising is to keep trying different approaches until you find the one or two that work for your product. In the case of my last business, which manufactures gas-monitoring instruments, we tried direct mail promotion, but it did not work. It did not even bring in sufficient responses from people who had specifically inquired to magazines after they saw our publicity releases about the products.

The publicity releases, however, did attract the attention of several important distributors. As another promotion test, we tried faxing introductory letters and a product flyer with a "special offer" to lists of members of a professional society. That promotion produced many sales. I think this approach worked because the professional society list was a very focused group in terms of interests, spending power and purchasing authority. However, I am not sure. That is why you have to keep trying promotional approaches in order to discover what will work for your particular niche.

Choosing the Right Distribution Channel

Finding the best way to deliver products to your customers is very important, but sometimes there is only one way in a traditional industry. For example, electrical supplies for home and commercial wiring, such as outlet boxes, are only available through retail outlets and electrical distributors. You cannot buy direct from the factory. This is changing in some industries because of the new marketing possibilities opened up by the 800 number and a Web site. Traditional distributors are either sinking or having to develop new strategies because of the profound changes in buying procedures caused by the Internet. Therefore, it is well worth your effort to find out what the current distribution channel for your product should be. Once you know that, you can then find out what distribution organizations you should contact. Research potential distribution methods and potential distributors carefully!

In many cases, distributors who become interested in a new company's product become key in at least the initial promotion of the products. My father developed the world's most popular bird feeder through his then-unknown company, Droll Yankees, Inc. He tried doing his own distribution in his home state of Rhode Island by selling directly to garden shops, farm feed stores and Audubon Society gift shops. The sales were not huge, but he was able to prove that he had a well-designed product at an acceptable price. A New Jersey distributor of home and garden products heard about his new line and asked whether he could show them at his booth in a New York trade show. The distributor received orders for 16,000 feeders, which at that time was beyond my father's wildest dreams. After that initial breakthrough, the business was able to expand its distribution to Abercrombie & Fitch, Orvis, Brookstone and other well-known specialty distributor/retailers.

My gas instrument business got its start when a local specialty distributor primed our pump. This distributor made significant sales for my start-up company. He specialized in instrumentation for medical sterilization equipment in the greater New York City market. He latched onto my product line and essentially saturated the New York market. Larger distributors, who sold many products to many kinds of customers over all the U.S. market, started approaching me. Because the instruments we manufactured are used in many industries and applications, I was able to broaden our distribution to nationwide and later worldwide customers. My company was underway! That first New York distributor kicked us off to a jackrabbit start by going into a market area I had hardly considered.

How a distributor can become a partner
Sometimes a good distribution relationship can become a business partnership or a contract management arrangement. My sister Anne Kilham, a successful artist producing gift cards featuring Maine coastal themes, told me how she became partners with her distributor:

> I had to admit to myself that I had made some bad choices in partners and associates. I think for most artistic types, business management is something we are unable to become good at. A person finally 'tapped' me at a trade show. He had been watching me for a while and decided that he could be of assistance in running my business. After a few months of negotiating we came to an agreement that has worked for the last 15 years. Mason Newick of Pen & Inc. manages my business, wholesale, retail mail order, negotiating, printing, manufacturing, warehousing, shipping and licensing. It is a unique arrangement and one that has worked very well for both of us.

My sister accomplished what many executives of much larger companies fail to do: she faced up to her limitations and was ready when someone found her and could make up for what she lacked as a businessperson. The result has been a very successful business.

The small business particularly can benefit from a "big brother" distributor who can take over more than just product distribution. Before signing an irrevocable agreement for such an arrangement, I recommend that you work for a 6-15 month "trial marriage" with the distributor without a binding agreement.

Shipping to and communicating with your distributors
Among the other things you need to consider in order to have a smoothly running distribution system is shipping. This may seem mundane, but it is extremely important to get right as soon as possible. Consider shipping boxes, cartons, or crates, as your case may be and try to use standard sizes that you can buy in quantity. Make sure they are compatible with volume shippers like UPS and Fed Ex.

Carton markings are important for efficient delivery and storage by your distributor. I have found, for example, that using bar codes is invaluable. We put bar code product stocking codes on cartons destined for our biggest and most automated distributors. Once we have bar coded the shipment, it can be laser scanned when it is delivered to the distributor. That way as soon as the goods arrive at the distributor's receiving dock, they can be automatically routed to the correct stocking position in the distributor's warehouse. Remember, your relationship with your distributor is a partnership where if you help the distributor to minimize their costs and maximize their customer service, they will prefer your products to those of a prospective competitive vendor. In the end, your customer will be better served.

My father was revolutionary in his day in communicating with distributors. He went from using the mails to Teletype. When I started in business, I began using faxes. My communications were document-oriented (i.e., forms, receipts, and invoices). Then I went to communicating with my suppliers and distributors by email. I have found that it is important to keep abreast of the latest communications technology as the speed of correspondence has become more and more a factor in the marketplace.

Establishing a Brand in the Marketplace

I opened this chapter by saying that customers buy satisfaction. I should add that in successful businesses more than 75% of sales come from established customers. Much of the remaining sales come from new customers who are referred by existing customers. This can happen when you have great products, great service, and a name or logo that is memorable. A logo therefore becomes the very essence of marketing the company and its products.

You want to create something that instantly pops into people's minds when they think about your type of products. When that happens, you know you have a successful brand! Think of Kleenex, Xerox or Coke as brands that come to mind for the generic product. You want as much as possible for your brand to become synonymous with the "right choice" for that kind of product.

Many entrepreneurs recognize the importance of establishing a brand, but they generally do not realize how fast a logo or name, casually or even accidentally established, catches on and becomes their brand, whether they like it or not. For this reason, from the day you start your business, you should have a trade name, logo and brand name ready to promote, before the market evolves one for you.

Developing a logo for your brand

I suggest starting by finding a name that is somewhat descriptive of your product or service and has a nice ring to it. Then check to see if someone else already has it trademarked. Make sure it is not too generic, like "Green Peas." If the name is memorable and OK to trademark, then proceed to have a logo designed. The logo usually is a stylized print representation of the brand. The logo can be trademarked if it is unique or specific and if no one else in your trade is using it. (See discussion of trademarks in chapter three.) The logo can be a stylized name like IBM, which stands for International Business Machines. It can be a design that suggests the name such as GE's logo, or it may be just an abstract symbol. The logo should be able to appeal to people of many countries because you may be exporting sooner than you imagined. It should also project well on everything from small business cards to trade show booths. Try cutting out logos of established brands to see what features the truly appealing ones have in common. Make sketches of potential logos that appeal to you. Try them out on family, friends and business associates.

My sister Anne, the artist in Maine, did the logo for Eco Sensors, Inc. It has the eye-catching color combination of orange, white and black. It combines a bird (the nighthawk, which is exceptionally sensitive to environmental changes) over an orange moon, and our name spelled out in stylized letters. It has received many compliments, stands out in a sea of logos, and prints equally well on our white letterhead paper or on our black instruments.

When you are satisfied with a general logo concept or design or even several possible ones, bring them to an artist. The artist may have interesting new logo designs to offer or may just do a final rendition of one of your designs. Almost all advertising agencies have logo creation specialists, and these agencies can be found in the Yellow Pages. You could also inquire about artists at art galleries, the art department of a local college, or through the suggestions of friends.

Protecting your trademark

After you have used a trademark or logo in commerce, the U.S. Department of Commerce will accept your application for a registered trademark. Your application will have to include samples of published product brochures or other commercial material that demonstrate your use of the trademark or logo in commerce. If you do not register your trademark, you can show that it is a trademark by putting TM after it. If your trademark is registered, it has more legal protection from infringement, and you can put ® after the trademark. (You will need to consult with an attorney who specializes in patents and trademarks for more complete information about this area.)

Publicizing Your New Business

Publicity can be a powerful tool for informing the marketplace about what you have to offer. Good publicity is definitely a marketing tool and a great stimulant for a business. How it is done and its scope depends on the nature of your business and the abilities of your key people. My father was a genius at gathering publicity for himself and his business. He was a colorful character and was known for telling old New England stories in a manner best described as "Yankee Talk." Newspapers loved his stories and his creative abilities. Therefore, they were willing to do stories about him regularly. Eventually a local NBC affiliate TV station discovered him and did a short report for one of their *Morning Magazine* programs. Their reporter interviewed him as he wandered around his shop, yard, and woods talking about birds and bird feeders. He projected well on TV. Later he would appear on the local public television station as an auctioneer for their fund raising benefits. A public awareness about him and his company developed. The *Droll Yankees* legend began.

I am not the colorful character my father was. Consequently, I have developed other business publicity approaches that emphasize my particular abilities. I try to get technical articles published in trade magazines, and I have become adept at giving technical presentations to trade groups in my market area. What I have found in common with my father's experience is that *favorable publicity thrives on personalities not companies.* I therefore encouraged the development of an image of myself as a creative leader in my area of environmental instrument design. As a result, my image became linked to my company and its products.

Other entrepreneurs I have known work better through promotion at the community level. Many of them accomplish this by working with charities, educational institutions, or other institutions to enhance their image and publicize their projects.

If you do not write articles yourself (or even if you do) try to get business and trade magazines, or even *Fortune* and *Business Week,* to do stories about you. If you have developed a breathtaking new mega technology these publications will pay attention. Once a publication believes they have discovered you, they can get very aggressive about getting your story out to the public.

Sometimes it is worth retaining a publicity agent. A good agent can often facilitate becoming "discovered" by important business publications. "PR people" are often part of advertising agencies, while others have their own small firms. The trick again is "research." Before concluding an agreement with a PR firm, get a list of their references and interview the references to see if the PR agent or firm has done well for someone like you in *your industry*.

Customer Feedback

One thing all successful businesses have in common is their commitment to carefully listening to their customers. Marketing and sales ought to generate for you a stream of information about your products and customer reactions. Use what you can to find out about the shortcomings of your products. This information can contribute to new ideas for new designs, for better marketing approaches and for new business opportunities.

Many smart chief executives of major corporations go on sales calls with salespeople many levels below them in the organization, just to gather information. They talk to passers-by at their company's trade show booths. They gather product and marketing ideas wherever they can and put them to use.

Every day at my office, I tried to take at least a few customer calls, even though there were apparently higher demands on my time. One customer call I took changed my company in a way I never could have predicted. He phoned and out of the blue said, "Did you know that your instruments can sense ozone?" I did not know. I was not even sure at that point what ozone was. Nevertheless, I figured I might have stumbled upon a hidden treasure. I looked into the customer's insight further. Sure enough, I found out that our instruments, while not designed to be sensitive to ozone, did sense it. I found out everything I could about ozone. I redesigned an instrument to be optimized for ozone detection and Voila! I had a ready market. Ozone eventually became the company's largest market.

It turned out that ozone is on everyone's mind wherever indoor air quality is a factor. *My company became the leader in simple, inexpensive ozone monitors for indoor use.* That bit of volunteered customer information became the tail that wagged the dog for my company. If I had not been willing to take that customer's call personally and listen to what he had to say, I would have missed a huge marketing and product area. Never underestimate your customers' responses to your products. You never know, until you listen, what treasures might be hidden there.

The Web and Your Business

One of the greatest marketing tools to come along in many years is the Worldwide Web. Upstart companies have become overnight miracles. Think of Amazon.com and eBay.com. They owe their existence to the Web. It is also very instrumental in perpetuating the leadership of such old-line retailers as L.L. Bean. This new resource can be equally important for entrepreneurs like you. It is of such importance that I will devote the entire next chapter to how to use the Web for your business.

7

THE LUCRATIVE WORLD OF
THE WEB

Give me a lever and I will move the world.
Archimedes

Suppose you could display your products to the whole world without advertising or trade shows. Everyone who mattered could instantly find out what you are selling. You could talk to any customer who showed interest in your display at virtually no cost to you. Well, this infinite display has arrived and its name is The Web. This maze of interconnecting computers is an on-demand information resource, a facility for making unlimited contacts and geared for free interaction. What most people do not realize is just how easy it is to establish a Web site, and how fast it can bring you results. For a modest investment, you can start a half-decent Web site. Forget about patents or a branch office in Atlanta. You may well get more out of an investment in a Web site.

I first saw the light by accident. We had a guesthouse for rent. Like everyone else in picturesque Santa Fe with a guesthouse, we advertised in the classified sections of the state tourist magazine and we enjoyed our share of guest responses. Then one day there was a solicitation in the mail for putting our guesthouse in a Vacation Rentals Web site. With no particular expectations, I sent the vacation rentals people some photos, a short description and about $50. The response was immediate. The Web site became our most effective guest producer.

Designing a Web site

If you are promoting anything from a book you wrote to an entire company and its range of products, you or the company will need a website. I realize that starting your site can seem like diving into a lake for the first time: it can look daunting at first. You will find, however, that once you are in, it feels great.

In the early days of the Web, it was almost impossible to develop your own website unless you were a skilled computer programmer. Now web "templates" are available, including with ready-made themes like a motel or a flower shop, where you can develop your own website. You compose text in Word, other text programs, or just type into the template. You can select from a wide variety of fonts and colors. Then you upload from your computer photos or other artwork to drop into the site.

Alternately, depending on your skills, time, and budget, you can engage a website developer to develop and maintain your website for you. Some are large nation organizations and some are locally oriented. Many have this as their "night job," working out of their home. I have used both, and either approach can work well. Now that I am out of industry and am writing books, I have developed my own website on Weebly, hosted by iPage.com, http://futurebooks.info.

You will need to purchase a "domain name," like future-books.info and this will be part of the "URL" like http://future-books.info. Domain names are supplied by specialty companies found on the Internet, and often by your web hosting company who represents a supplier. In any case, they are typically $10 to $20 per year. The web hosting itself can range from almost nothing to hundreds of dollars per year. For a simple website, you should estimate $50 per year.

You should also find and install one or more website statistics ("webstats") tracking apps. Often your web host will have one as part of their package. I have tried many and recommend statcounter.com. It is simple but offers a wide range of statistic with heavy emphasis on the visitors: who they are, where they are (pins on a map), what pages in your site they visited, how long they were on the pages, their search terms to find you, traffic trends over time, and more. This information is vital in both understanding your market and editing your website.

My Company's Early Experience with a Website

About a month after Eco Sensors submitted search terms and received our domain name, we started receiving inquiries from visitors who toured our Website. Some of these contacts were by an inquiry form found on our Web site. This form sent the inquiries to our e-mail address. Other visitors e-mailed us directly. They could also phone or fax. All this information was on our Web site.

What quickly caught my attention was the very high rate of *conversion to sales* received through our Web site. About 25% of the prospective customers who inquired about our products, after browsing our site, bought from us. A typical buyer could be a project engineer for an electrical generating plant. This engineer would be looking for a detector for the ozone given off by his generators. When he logged on, he had no idea who made such equipment. Using a search engine on the Web, the engineer could enter such search terms as "ozone," "detection," and "portable." The search engine displays six companies with products that fit these terms. The engineer then visits those companies' Web sites and by comparing their offerings to his needs, narrows the search further. There is my company, Eco Sensors, and other prospective vendors. The engineer efficiently finds what he is looking for, and before he loses interest or is sidetracked by another project, he contacts the suppliers. An experienced Web cruiser can do the entire search and find operation in less than 25 minutes.

Using traditional sales methods, the same project engineer mentioned above would shuffle through brochures left by sales representatives, thumb through back issues of trade magazines, and consult standard industrial product source directories, many of which are thick volumes. He might get tired, confused, and distracted by other projects. Finally, he might send out inquiries for more information to any potential supplier who appears vaguely qualified. It should come as no surprise that after all this a conversion rate of *inquiries to sales* is typically about 3%, instead of the roughly 25% we've experienced from Web buyers.

Why is the website so much more effective? My explanation is that the people who take the trouble to find a website, explore it, and then contact you, are very focused. They have a buying commitment in mind before they start the search. On the other hand, people who respond to advertisements in trade magazines by information return cards usually are not serious buyers. It is easy, it passes the time, and they can gather and file information for some vague future reference.

On the other hand, if they visit the supplier's website found in the ad, the advertisement is effective and worthwhile for all concerned.

Web Sites vs. Advertisements

Web sites should present much more information than advertisements. You are not being charged for space you occupy with your Web site. You are being charged for every tiny bit of space used in advertisements. (There are slight extra charges for very large amounts of Web space used.) Utilize the free space of your Web site to put in as many pages as you like about applications for your products ("app notes") as well as the use and maintenance of your products ("tech notes"). You are in effect giving information away in order to generate interest in your products and to encourage buyers who have suitable applications for your products. You are also qualifying your company as The Authoritative Source. This approach is being exploited all over the Web. For example, visit Amazon.com's Web bookstore and see the large amounts of information they offer. They will post several reviews and reader's comments even for minor books. Amazon.com also makes finding books easy because the books are cross-referenced in many different ways.

Getting Paid for Web Transactions

Because the Web produces enthusiastic, even impassioned buyers, they will want to consummate their purchase without further delay. They will not want to wait for research on their credit worthiness. They will be aggravated by receiving your shipment COD. This means that to be a serious Web merchant, you must accept major credit cards. They are the basis for most cyber transactions.

Unfortunately, for a small or start-up company, it can be difficult to be approved as a credit card merchant. The process is a little like looking for a loan: you just keep knocking on doors until someone agrees to approve you. If a bank has known you personally for at least three years, that is a good place to start. All of this foot-dragging is because legally your little company is liable for its bad credit card transactions (invalid credit card or a customer who changes his mind after the transaction). If you do not have the resources and intent to cover this bad credit card risk, the prospective credit card processing institutions lose interest.

Because Internet transactions are not in person, you process these by some sort of terminal. The old way was by multipart forms you took to the bank every day. Very cumbersome for you and the bank. You can use a card-swipe terminal with keyboard and digital readouts, just like the ones you see in stores. These are very nice, but they are expensive and space consuming, so you can use a little-known method called ARU (nobody knows what that stands for). With this method, you enter the customer's card information and amount of the transaction into your touch-tone phone. Almost instantly, you receive an approval code. Then the amount of the transaction is electronically forwarded to your bank account. We progressed to an on-line program linked to software in our computer. The program carries out and records the credit card transactions. Credit card processing, including verification, will continue to evolve. Many of the coming systems will be based on the smartphone as a terminal.

Payment by Government Agencies and Foreign Customers

Over half of our foreign customers paid by credit card—even for orders of up to $10,000. This method is so much simpler than processing letters of credit, foreign checks, or bank drafts. In the United States, government agencies and large corporations are rapidly going to credit cards for purchases of up to $5,000 or so. The Federal Government Visa Card is a tangible benefit of the Paperwork Reduction Act. The traditional method of purchase for a government agency buyer was to ask you to mail them a quote. After they received it, they would then mail out requests for bids. If you won, they would mail you a purchase order, and you would send them your product and mail duplicate copies of your invoice. A month or more later, if all went well, you would receive a check. With the Federal Visa Card, if the government buyer is convinced yours is the right product for the application, he or she gives you the Visa Card number and says, "Ship it."

The Web and Distributors

The use of Web site marketing is destroying the traditional concepts of marketing by territory. Previously, salespeople, representatives and distributors would have territories such as counties, states, or countries. Now, information leaps whole oceans and continents in a microsecond. People everywhere want a better deal by going directly to the manufacturers or by dealing with a more informed distributor. Middleman distributors who survive this technological shift will be forced to maintain reasonable margins, be well informed about their products, and have very accessible and useable (and often multilingual) Web sites.

At Eco Sensors, we found that our distributors who did not have first class Web sites fell behind. The distributors that do have effective Web sites are doing better than ever. A new development is that distributors are selling over territory and country lines. Our best distributor in France is in Montreal, Canada. He has a good French language Web site, and therefore French buyers in both Canada and France patronize him.

During a recent trip to Japan, I was making conversation with a young Japanese commuter on a train. I asked if he used the Internet. He said "yes" because he belonged to a weekend U.S. country-style music band. "What?" I said. He explained that his band used to buy Japanese electric guitars even though they thought the American electric guitar was a better product. The advent of the Internet allowed these Japanese singing cowboys to order parts for their American guitars directly, cheaply and easily. They would log on to the U.S. parts supplier, give their order, credit card number, address, and get their needed supplies. As a result, they are switching back to American guitars.

The Website as a Service Center

Our Web site was originally conceived to support our existing customers and distributors. I did not envision it principally as a sales medium to prospective customers. It has proved to be both. As originally conceived, the Eco Sensors site provides general product information but no prices. It contains a growing library of applications and service information. People who own or sell our products can log-on to the Eco Sensors Web site any time, and they get the product applications and support information they require. There are simple diagnostic and repair procedures for our products, applications notes and other information to help users in the field.

I think of it as similar to the customer who buys a home appliance. They want to be able to find usage and technical information about the appliance in the manufacturer's Web site. Not only would the consumer potentially use this information (because breakdowns invariably occur on weekends when service is unavailable), but this information would also be available to the appliance dealer's technicians. If you knew such a resource was available, you might well be more likely to buy that brand of appliance. That is how my service-oriented Web site has again become a sales tool.

Using a Website to Attract Big Buyers

Contrary to my original expectations, my Web site tends to attract buyers in the larger corporations and government agencies. They prowl around in cyberspace looking for the right product at the right price for their agency or company. To help them find you in their search, it is a good idea to get your Web site listed in "product locator" Web sites maintained by trade magazines. There they can find your company's listing and Web site address using search terms. This indexing of information on companies of all sizes is also happening with general industrial product source directories, such as Thomas Register. The Eco Sensors Web site is referenced by search terms on the Thomas Register Website, and through this route, we have received many quality inquiries and sales.

Maximizing Your Website Success

Here are some other considerations to maximize your success with a Website and e-mail communication:

- Start immediately with your own short, preferably single word site name, such as Birds.com if you are going to be a birdseed supplier. Do not try to economize by being a file extension of someone else's domain name such as CapeCodNet.com/Birds. Eventually you will have your own domain name anyway. Once you do, you will find that untangling the old Web site name and getting everyone to know your new Web site name through all the search engines, directories, and customer files, will be a monumental and frustrating task.

- Get on lots of search engines. Get listed in the "product locator" specialty Web sites that reference other Web sites. Your Internet Service Provider can get you listed with the search engines. If not, they should be able to refer you to specialty firms who provide this service. The product locator Web sites are generally advertised in trade magazines for the target market of interest.

- Get the best computer, modem, network, and software packages you can afford. When you really get rolling, system speed and large memory become essential. Most small businesses use their main PC for several roles, such as word processing, accounting, and Internet access. The problems start if the computer is taking a long time to process all the e-mails of the day. There will not be time left over for accounting and other tasks. The more sophisticated computers and software do not mind running several programs at once (such as the accounting program asked to standby, while the Internet e-mail program is running). Lesser systems tend to get all fouled up so that computer "crashes" or system "lockups" become common. If you are very attached to your present system, consider a second system just for e-mails and Web responses.

• Work cooperatively with your distributors who have Websites so that you are partners, not competitors. This might mean quickly answering their requests for product shipments and information, giving them support text and graphics for their Websites. In some cases, it may be desirable to have your customers "jump" to your distributors' Web sites by clicking on their site name in your Website. For example, German customers can jump to your German distributor and vice versa. This is very easy for your Internet Service Provider or your Web Master to program for you. It is a worthwhile addition to your Web site.

Undoubtedly, the costs of Web marketing will increase as the providers of Web access products and services experiment with higher pricing. We can expect government agencies to find ways to tax cyberspace transactions. Nevertheless, the Web is the greatest marketing, sales, and service tool of our time, especially for the small business entrepreneur. You can easily spread awareness of your products, brands and company to millions or even billions of people. You can take orders from anywhere, and your customers are more professionally serviced by the information they can find on your site. The Web is the best thing to come along in years, primarily because it levels the playing field between you and the mega-corporations.

Now that we have explored cyberspace and the Web, it is time to come back to earth and explore how to manufacture the products you will sell on the Web.

8

SUCCESSFULLY MANUFACTURING YOUR PRODUCT

For want of a nail...the battle was lost.
Anon.

I have seen a lot of promising businesses go off the rails because of misunderstandings about manufacturing. The manufacturing process as it applies to your product needs careful analysis. Every detail, every step, all procedures, all costs, all time sequences, all suppliers, all testing and more must be researched and documented. When I look for someone to manufacture something, I look for someone who loves details because the devil is in the details of manufacturing.

One of your first basic decisions is what manufacturing you will do yourself.

Deciding What You Need to Manufacture In-House

The first reality of do-it-yourself manufacturing is that it often requires very high capital investment. This stark fact of life eliminates many of the things you might like to manufacture yourself. If your dream is the assembly of simple but state-of-the-art electronic products, then a couple of million dollars must be found to build and equip a plant. If you want to make semiconductor chips, you will need ten billion dollars to build and equip a basic plant. These are extreme examples, but you get the idea.

It has been my experience that this investment in manufacturing is not the best use of capital for most start-up companies. The available funds can be better used for product development and marketing. If you can find suitable contract manufacturers for your products and you feel confident you can manage them even though they are not in your personal factory, you might seriously consider this option. For three generations of my family, our most successful ventures were "manufacturing" products that actually were contracted out.

>>> *Contract manufacturers do not need to be nearby to be the right ones for you and being distant need not be an important drawback. My grandfather's oil burner business in New Mexico used a manufacturer in Columbus, Ohio. Today with comprehensive and low cost communications facilitated by e-mail, high-speed direct data transmission, and video conferencing, relative locations are only limited by the bounds of cyberspace.*

Even huge companies face the make-or-buy decision. Sony, for instance, has not made most of its electronic products. It purchased them from contract suppliers, although this policy may have changed. On the other hand, IBM did all its own manufacturing for years. It purchased product from outside only relatively recently. As I write, it has put its semiconductor chip manufacturing facility up for sale. Both companies are successful, so either approach can work.

GREAT IDEA TO A GREAT COMPANY

Trying to Rejuvenate an Old Factory - How I Saw the Light

Several companies ago in about 1980, I was hired to run the plastics machinery manufacturing subsidiary of a large conglomerate. When I came in, it was explained to me that the subsidiary I would be running had been losing money habitually. The plastics machines it produced, primarily extruders, were still much respected in its industry. The company was sure that an energetic young man such as me could turn it around. I did not have much time to check out the company when they hastened my acceptance of the job with a generous offer.

The plant I was to take charge of sprawled over the better part of a city block in an old industrial section of New Jersey. On my first day of work as I started walking down the weedy walk to the front door, I noticed faces peering at me from the upper windows of the "executive office building." There was a great deal of mutual curiosity. After I made it through the waiting room full of faded and cracked pictures of long discontinued machinery, I found myself in my new home, the General Manager's office. I was thinking to myself, "I'm walking into a backward and dusty time-warp, but if I work hard I can turn it around."

My first contact was with the young woman operating the telephone switchboard. There was no cell phone, no Internet. You just told Barbara whom you wanted to talk to, and she connected you. She waited attentively to see whom I might place my first call to. Then I was shown to my office. It was completely wood paneled and had its own little bathroom. It was furnished with a glass top mahogany desk with a few screws missing. It had padded leather chairs whose springs were beginning to show.

The word was out that I was looking around, so when I strolled through the attached factory I found gritty operators

and their machining and welding steel. The shop superintendent and his foremen huddled intently over blueprints. In a
few days, I decided that the employees were a nice family of
people who had worked together for years.

I tried everything to turn this lovable old place around.
I got rid of some deadwood front office personnel. I initi-
ated new product designs and new sales initiatives, but the
losses persisted. The parent conglomerate had really let this
company go to seed. Necessary investment in new plant and
equipment had been neglected for too long. After three years
of unprofitable operation under my command, the parent
company decided that the subsidiary should be sold. I made
a meager offer, and they accepted, happy to dump their white
elephant on me.

With only limited cash resources, I had no time to lose. My
only option was to contract out manufacturing. This was an
approach the old parent company had felt was unacceptable.
I gave everyone in the shop their last paycheck and sent out
piles of blueprints to potential bidders for machinery building contracts. These were sent to three experienced machinery builders with much more modern plant and equipment
facilities. All the offers I received were at least 25% below our
previous costs to manufacture the identical products ourselves!
This included contract manufacturer's profits! Furthermore,
my new company's cash flow would be improved because we
were paying for the outside-produced machinery *after* delivery.
Previously, we had been paying for our machinery products
before delivery. We had to buy steel, pay for rent and payroll,
and so forth before completing the products. This manufacturing outsourcing strategy was a great success, and I have used it
many times since.

Manufacturing Analysis for Your Products

No two manufacturing situations are entirely similar. Rarely can manufacturing of technical products be set up from a simple recipe. My experience has shown me that determining an effective manufacturing strategy requires considerable study.

In considering how you are going to do your manufacturing, the decision criteria you should use include:

- How many units to produce.
- How much capital needs to be allocated to manufacturing.
- Whether to license or contract out your manufacturing.

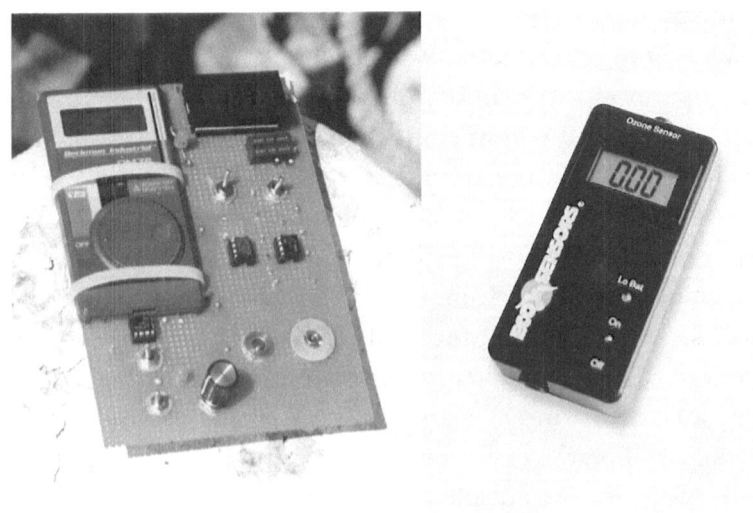

My Eco Sensors, Inc., ozone sensing instrument. The 1991 hand-made developmental model and an easily manufactured fourth-generation commercial version, 2000.

How many units to produce

How many units of a product you make each year or your annual production volume is a very important consideration in deciding where and how to manufacture. You are more likely to interest an outside manufacturer if you will be producing dozens to hundreds of units per year with no changes in the design. The more you produce, the greater the cost savings. These potential cost savings are often best realized by a contract manufacturer who has invested in costly mass-production manufacturing equipment. His or her manufacturing cost savings would of course be passed on to you.

On the other hand, if you are going to make 2-5 big systems a year, doing your own manufacturing probably is best. Limited production of large and complex products often means that they are at least partially custom-built to customer specifications. However, I have successfully contracted out the manufacturing of one-of-a-kind large machines. When I did, I had complete parts lists and drawings. In addition, there were several qualified and interested manufacturers nearby to do the work. There are problems in low volume manufacturing, however.

Low volume manufacturing problems

People who start technical businesses often do not realize how important volume production is in achieving consistent profitability. My father owned a company in the 1950s and 60s that manufactured sophisticated metal bending machines based on his patented designs. Because he would only make a dozen or so machines each year of each model, he made them in his shop. It was a pleasant environment with a couple of faithful workers working with him. His machine shop was located on a picturesque corner of our farm. The business was his dream realized. However, he had not addressed profitability through volume production, and the business eventually folded.

My father then went on to a high-volume business. He had bird feeders made from his own designs and used a contract manufacturer to do the work. Unlike the low volume metal bending machines, the bird feeders were highly profitable almost from the beginning.

The case for doing your own manufacturing

In the start-up stages of most businesses, capital is usually in very short supply; yet that is when the outlay of capital for manufacturing space and equipment is often at its greatest. If you invest in a state-of-the-art manufacturing plant, you may have little resources left for engineering, marketing and administration. Also, even manufacturing medium-technology products usually requires a wide range of specially trained people who can be both difficult to find when you need them and hard to afford.

In spite of all these drawbacks and considerations, there are persuasive reasons for doing your own manufacturing. These include:

- You have more control over the way your products are manufactured.
- You have more control over product quality.
- You can more easily use secret formulas and manufacturing methods.
- You may also seek to use your plant as a laboratory to develop additional proprietary manufacturing methods.

A semi-manufacturing concept that I used is having an outside contractor do the basic manufacturing while maintaining my own shop for manufacturing support. I used my shop to:

- Engineer the product for the lowest cost manufacturing.
- Prepare and document manufacturing methods and instructions for the contract manufacturer.
- Keep special and proprietary parts until the manufacturer needs them.

My shop also received the finished goods from the manufacturer. At that point, I used my shop to:

- Inspect the incoming products. I make notes about quality. Also, this is a time when slight revisions to the products can be made to improve their appearance or operating characteristics.
- Do any customizations for particular customers.
- Calibrate instruments.
- Package and inventory the finished goods.
- Ship orders to customers.
- Repair and return customers' products that have developed problems.

This approach is a good compromise between controlling your own manufacturing and having a professional manufacturer sweat out the details. It also gives your customers the comforting feeling that you are a real "manufacturer" and not a virtual company merely acting as a sales agent for a low cost manufacturer elsewhere.

Licensing out your manufacturing

Another approach to minimizing manufacturing capital is to license someone else to manufacture your products. The licensed manufacturer can produce your product either for their own use or to sell to your customers. The legal distinction between licensed manufacturing and contract manufacturing is that for licensing you do not own the products after they are manufactured. You own the designs, patents and know-how, and the licensed manufacturer owns the finished products for sale. My grandfather did this very successfully in the 1930s through the 1950s with his oil burners for home use. The burners used his patented designs for home furnaces and hot water heaters. However, my grandfather never made them or even saw them. The burners were manufactured and sold by a company in Ohio that paid royalties to my grandfather's company. In his best years, the licensee would sell over a million burners a year just to Sears.

Financial Considerations of Licensing vs. Direct Manufacturing

Financial

The advantage of the licensing approach for my grandfather was that he did not have to tie up his capital in manufacturing. He also did not have to worry about the details of manufacturing and sales. He lived a good life as a successful inventor and country gentleman on his oil burner royalties.

On the other hand, if he had used a contract manufacturer, his "bottom line" profits would have been several times larger than the royalties he received for his inventions. Royalties are usually calculated as a percentage of sales and are typically only one quarter to one half of the pretax profits of products you would have manufactured yourself or by way of contractors.

Patents

Licensing works reasonably well as long as long as your patents are valid. But as the patents expire, the pressure is on to find new variations of the products to patent in order to protect your licenses. My grandfather wound up with more than 100 patents on his oil burners. Today the cost of patents is many times higher than in my grandfather's time. The cost of getting a new patent can exceed $8,000. So entrepreneurs today are thinking much more carefully before investing in patents. In many cases, it is better to get into production quickly without losing the time the patenting process often entails.

Brand name considerations

Another potential disadvantage of the licensing approach is that you usually are not in a position to build up your own brand name. When my grandfather was nearing retirement age (although people like him never fully retire), and his designs were becoming technically obsolete, his business rapidly lost value. This was because his business had very little brand or trade name recognition. With no new products and patents, the business sank almost without a trace. If he had developed a strong brand by controlling his own manufacturing and marketing, he could have used that brand to help buy other companies or product lines. That would have enabled him to assure the continuance of his company after his retirement. If he had wanted to sell his company instead, he would have been able to command a much higher price if his company was synonymous with a strong brand.

I was a director of a small company with patented technology for airbags. These devices control airbags in automobile crashes so that they will not deploy too rapidly and injure the occupants. We licensed our inventions to automobile manufacturers through their suppliers. Without the continuing stream of improvement patents we keep developing, we would soon be out of business. I knew that if we did not develop a strong brand name for some of our own manufactured products, it would be difficult to sell our business for a premium price in the future. We looked for some product that we could manufacture and market ourselves to form the basis for building our own brand name but did not find any that seemed right. We sold the company for the value of its intellectual property (IP), the patents and know-how.

Managing Working Capital

So far, in my discussions about manufacturing capital, I have been talking about fixed capital. Fixed capital is your investment in plant, equipment, and other more or less permanent assets. The other kind of capital that warrants your consideration is working capital for manufacturing. Working capital is the cash you use to buy raw materials, outside manufactured products and manufacturing services, pay your manufacturing payroll and other costs associated with manufacturing, such as rent and utilities.

You need to analyze all your options to see how you can minimize the amount of working capital you will have to tie up in manufacturing. Will you tie up less working capital doing your own manufacturing or using a contract manufacturer? Much of this calculation depends on when you have to pay for inventory and manufacturing services in relation to when you are paid for the products you ship.

Obviously, if you can pre-sell your manufactured products, you may not have to tie up any working capital. This is called "JIT" or "just in time" inventory purchasing. You manufacture or purchase just when the products must be shipped. The Japanese are past masters of this technique and much of their industry works this way. Successful JIT manufacturing depends on you having an easily manufactured standard product. It also is important to have a marketing department which sells against just available production. They exhort customers to buy whatever is coming off the production line—this week it is blue cars.

One problem that develops with JIT manufacturing is unexpected parts shortages. I discovered at my environmental instrument company where we practiced JIT to some extent, that if there is a parts shortage, my production at the contract manufacturer is delayed. This delays my pre-sold deliveries to customers. As a result, I lose valuable goodwill with customers, orders are canceled, and my cash position drops. Because our instrumentation used a lot of electronic components such as semiconductor "chips," an unexpected strike at a chip plant in Asia or the appearance of a mega-buyer entering the market and gobbling up chips en masse, can ruin my company's best-laid plans. Therefore, JIT manufacturing is best for markets where customers do not mind if there are some production delays.

Developing Manufacturing Secrets Protection

Many businesses are started based on secret know-how in manufacturing. Perhaps the most famous is Coca Cola with their still-secret recipe for Coke syrup. I believe every manufacturing process has possibilities for secrets to protect itself from easy copying by competitors. Almost all food and beverage creations are alleged to have secret formulations. (Even McDonald's claims to have a secret sauce on its hamburgers.)

In electronics, it is more difficult to hide proprietary know-how. However, if software is involved, secrets can be "embedded" in special microprocessor chips. This is probably the simplest way to hide secrets for the small electronics developer. Mechanical engineering relies on proprietary special metal alloys, other material formulations, and secret manufacturing methods.

In an earlier company I owned, Flow Vision, much of my real proprietary strength, apart from two patents, were the secret methods I used for bonding sapphires and diamonds to special steels. The sapphires and diamonds were used as super high strength windows through which to observe hostile chemical processes. This was one area I took care not to describe in the patents! Patents are public record, and anything you disclose in your patent is on display for the whole world to know. You only disclose in your patent what needs to be disclosed, such as demonstration of a novel idea reduced to practice, but not any additional information that may be crucial to your process.

In a more down-to-earth and common example, my sister Anne Kilham has a business producing Maine coast theme gift cards. The cards are based on block prints and paintings. In order to make more attractive cards than the competition, she started out using special inks and papers. Anne personally purchased the inks and papers, and she supervised the card printing at a local printer who she selected for his careful artisanship. They developed a valuable pool of special expertise together. But publishing and printing technology has changed radically in the last few years. Now she says that the printing is done by a computerized process, although still on art paper, and the process is less craft and more science. Nevertheless, Anne is developing specialty expertise which can be valuable in protecting her business.

You would be surprised at what the outside world finds unfathomable about the manufacturing of various products. Sometimes, what seems rather obvious to you can baffle teams of outside experts trying to "reverse engineer" your process to figure out your methods. They may not know, for instance, all the variables involved in your manufacturing process or how to calibrate and test the finished products.

In my environmental monitoring instrument business, we purchased gas sensors from standard industry suppliers. Although our electronic designs were imaginative, they were not proprietary. We have found that our greatest protection from would-be copiers was our secret calibration procedures. To make my environmental sensors work correctly requires a unique system. Certain gases require special and expensive calibration equipment and special techniques that we have mastered over the years. Potential competitors either do not have the patience to learn and apply advanced calibration techniques, or they do not want to become involved with prod-ucts where tedious and expensive calibration techniques are involved. Whatever the case, so far, my company's calibration systems have kept their product safe from copiers.

Keeping your secrets

One of the major concerns for any new technology company is that the employees, when they leave the company to work for someone else or start their own business, will use the know-how that they have learned from you. For this reason there are "non-compete agreements" to help you protect your business secrets. Unfortunately, these agreements are not always fully enforceable. In a trial today's liberal judges may "red line" or cross out sections of the agreement that are considered too onerous or restrictive. This is true especially as it affects the junior employees who have left your company and who claim to be just pursuing betterment in their trade.

I have found that the best defense against damaging employee defections is to keep secret from them the sources of key raw materials or key vendors. I may also sign exclusive supplier agreements with key vendors. As a general rule, it is best that employees intimately involved with production details should not have in-depth knowledge of customers as well. You do not want the business to walk out of the door in the minds of one or two people. When first starting a company, this may all sound very duplicitous to you. I realize that in the beginning, everyone is excited and the honeymoon is on. And that is as it should be. Still, as an entrepreneur you cannot afford to jeopardize your future. You must protect your own interests because when you do you are also effectively assuring the long-term job security of your permanent employees as well.

Controlling the Details

One reason people do their own manufacturing is because they can work out the product design and manufacturing details along the way. When the need arises, they can improvise. In addition, manufacturing is ideally suited for people who love both control and details. Most products today, from chocolate chip cookies to automobiles, require from dozens to thousands of ingredients, components or parts. Often, if one part is missing, production halts. It is like the old story about "for want of a nail the shoe was lost, for want of a shoe the horse was lost, for want of a horse, the rider was lost, and for want of a rider the battle was lost." Therefore, before the battle someone has to make sure that all the horseshoes are nailed on. In a modern enterprise that person is the production manager, VP of manufacturing, or most likely in a small start-up company, you.

You can figure out a way to make a nail so that the battle will not be lost. But unless shop floor improvisation is what you want out of life, it is an inefficient way to manage a company. It is better to develop complete and thorough documentation of your products as well as their manufacturing processes. In the end, this is your best assurance of quality and consistency in your product.

Production manufacturing documentation should include:

- **Parts or ingredient lists**. Show parts, part numbers, vendors, vendor part numbers, and costs. There should also be accompanying drawings showing, naming, and numbering parts and their assembly. This should also include software listings or sources if coding is embedded in your products.
- **Photos showing correctly produced products** as well as key steps along the way.
- **Lists of machine times and labor hours** needed for each manufacturing step in order to produce your product.

Controlling Quality

Business and non-business writers alike have struggled for years to define "quality." You might ask, "If it is such an elusive parameter, how do you control it?" There are two ways to approach quality control. One is the old time common sense "You know it when you see it." The other is "statistical" quality control. Often they wind up being almost the same thing.

You know quality when you see it

"You know it when you see it" is the old fashioned answer, and it is still useful. A sample of a product may pass all engineering tests but for some reason may just look wrong. Something is a little crooked, a weld does not seem solid, and a wire is dangling. These are signs to customers that dedication to quality is slipping. Workmanship is perfunctory. It calls to mind the story about the surgeon leaving a sponge in the patient. The competitors' salespeople are usually quick to learn about your quality problems, and they spread the word.

"Management by walking around" is a powerful management tool. When I ran the machinery manufacturing plant in New Jersey mentioned earlier in this chapter, I would walk the plant every day. I would stop and chat with a machinist here, a welder there. I would be conspicuously seen stopping to inspect machines in the final stages of manufacturing. I would run my fingers along the welds and check out the paint jobs. I looked for poorly finished machinery. This was the shop superintendent's job, but I wanted to be seen as a chief executive who cared about his plant's products. I also wanted my employees to know that I cared about what left the shop under our name.

This kind of approach not only affects quality control, but it can also be the kind of involvement with your product that stimulates that extra effort on the part of your employees. After all, if you do not care, neither will they. It is also important to compliment jobs well done and not just be finding fault.

This also prompts better workmanship and a greater sense of involvement.

Statistical quality control

In the technological world we live in, quality control is more often done by statistical methods. These measurements can show trends of deviation from a quality goal. You count how many and what kind of defects there are per batch of products produced, and then you seek out manufacturing remedies based upon the defect patterns that emerge with this method. If you find deviation from a quality norm, you can determine what flawed part or procedure is causing the problem. You can then take remedial action, such as letting a vendor know that his part or service is faulty.

ISO 9000 certification

Major buyers and government agencies are increasingly insisting on certification of quality control methods before you are qualified as a vendor. The small start-up business often cannot avoid these statistical quality control procedures, however onerous they may seem. Our document-crazy society wants traceability for everything. Think about what the plaintiff's lawyer can do to you in a product liability trial if you do not have substantial quality control documentation. For these reasons, the ISO has come into being.

The ISO (International Standards Organization) has the most widely used quality certification. It is called ISO 9000 (and its variations). Having an ISO 9000 certificate has become increasingly necessary for selling to governments and large corporations.

As a small start-up company, you will not need to apply for ISO 9000 right away. Approval usually takes several years of training, instituting procedures, and passing inspections, and the costs can mount into the thousands of dollars. You have to start somewhere though. By instituting good quality control procedures and documentation, you are ever closer to your ISO 9000 approval. From the start, you will be instilling the importance of quality into your organization.

After you have settled on your manufacturing approach, you are now ready to look at all the resources that you will need to make your company work. I will discuss this in the next chapter.

9

MARSHALING YOUR RESOURCES

Noah: "I ain't got much, but I'm all I got."
God: "Take what you've got and do what you can."
Old Song

Resource analysis is a very important part of your business plan. Therefore, think of all the resources or assets that will contribute to the success of your business. (For simplicity, in this chapter, I will use "resources" to mean resources or assets.) There are obvious things such as the room available for the business in your house or a nice car that will impress clients. Doubtless, there you will have other significant resources. It is important to know and be able to list all your resources. This ability demonstrates that you have a) the necessary resources to start the business, b) that you know which ones are missing and c) that you know where to get them. Making this list should also show that you know the costs of your yet unacquired resources. (All foreseeable expenditures for resources need to be included in your business plan.)

Again and again, I have seen resources overlooked which turn out to be key to a company's success. In two of the companies I founded, I discovered that obscure technical literature, filed away long ago because it seemed to have no immediate purpose, had critical information necessary for the design of my new products. This was quite a boon because one was a file on specialty fiber optics manufacturers, and the other was a manufacturer's technical data sheet for the use of their miniature amplifiers. These were essential because I was designing a new chemical monitoring instrument using new combinations of fiber optics and miniature amplifiers.

The key resources you should be thinking about are:

- Cash
- Technical and market information
- People and contacts
- Cooperative development and strategic alliances
- Franchises and licenses
- Buildings and space
- Machinery and equipment
- Computers and software
- Credit cards

Of all your resources, the most tangible is cash. Without cash everything stops. Everyone knows this and tries to start a business with enough cash. Unfortunately, there always seems to be less of it than your most pessimistic scenario. Why can your assumed cash hoard shrink so fast?

- **Some investor's cash does not show up.** There are always investors who like to operate by attaching conditions at the last minute such as investment installments according to performance. In theory, they may have a point, but it starts you off in a weakened position.

- **Endless deposits and advance payments** The utility companies all want deposits for a year or two when you are least able to pay. Realizing your tenuous longevity is of course why they do this. But this is often a shock to people who are used to consumer hookups without deposits. Different rules. Professionals who provide services such as legal and advertising are more likely to ask a start-up company for advances (or "retainers") than they would for established firms.

- **Slower receivables collection than planned**. Receivables are the monies owing to you by customers. The theory is that these all show up and are useable in 30 days. With all the delays that can accumulate, of which the mail is only one, 45 days is more realistic. Some customers have problems of their own and timely payment of their vendors becomes an act of denial. These are the sort of people who stall payment of the final installment of progress payments based on the slightest excuse. For all these reasons, I strongly recommend that the start-up business get set up as soon as possible to receive customers' payments by credit card. Of course, there is a several percent fee to pay for each transaction, but this will look like a good expenditure in retrospect.

- **Project delays.** For whatever reasons, major fabrication projects such as building major equipment never seem to be completed on time. Meanwhile, the employees and the rent must be paid on time, so the cash position erodes further.

- **Change of employees.** After an employee quits, there usually is severance pay which is a non-productive expense, and the pay for the replacement employee which is non-productive until he learns his job. New businesses often experience high employee turnover until things settle down.

- **Purchases of excess inventory.** A common mistake of new businesses is to buy more inventory than they need in fear of running out in a critical customer situation. Most customers would prefer that you remain solvent and a valued supplier than to have inventory-related shipping delays now and then.

This list of unexpected cash drains goes on and on, so it should be no surprise that most start-up companies run out of cash from their first round of financing. For this reason, many venture capital firms set up a reserve for each investment at least equal to that investment.

In monitoring the progress of my companies, I like to use the "Doomsday Ratio." This is the current amount of cash in the company's bank account divided by the average cash consumption per month. The resulting ratio is the number of months to insolvency if no more receivables are collected (which is quite possible if there are long dry spells in sales or collections as can happen to start-up companies selling large systems or package deals). To interpret the ratios, I use the following experienced-based rules:

- Over 6 months: generally a comfortable cushion.
- 4-6 months: a desirable target range.
- 2-4 months: probably adequate if the business is generally profitable and has consistent sales at good gross margins (50% or more).

- Less than 2 months: The situation is probably critical, and full attention should be focused on increasing liquidity.

Cash is great, and extra cash gives you bargaining options, new project funds, and so on, that your competition may not have. But cash is not the only resource for your attention.

It is important to identify carefully all the resources you will need and to acquire the first stage critical ones in the beginning. After that, keeping an eye on your resources becomes one of your most important tasks. Here are other resources for your attention.

Technical and Market Information

Good technical data and market information are powerful resources for a new business. I have run across countless technically based companies who seem to have discovered their lack of this information a few months into operations. They found they had no exact recipes for building their products; they did not know how to test their products; or they had only a vague idea of the size and characteristics of their market. In a very competitive world, no business can afford to be vague in these matters.

Technical and market information that is focused and specifically useful for your company is bound to be hard to find, even via that new savior, the Internet. (This is one reason why so many company employment agreements are the most restrictive about divulging the trade secrets and customer and market data. You just do not realize how valuable this information is until your competitors have it).

To start, you must have an outline of what information package you would like to assemble. For instance, if you are starting a biochemical business, you will need a lot of information relating to biochemical products and their uses. Much of this type of information can be found in back issues of trade magazines and technical journals. Begin by sorting through many trade magazines, brochures, and so forth, to extract the pieces of information you need to assemble your information package.

Trade magazines and manufacturers' product information packages are often the best sources. They can provide specific information relating to small specialty or "niche" market opportunities. These publications are often available in the larger libraries. Backdate issues can also be found in the libraries of specialized departments at colleges, universities and government agencies.

When I began my environmental instrument company, I reviewed environmental, scientific and trade publications pertaining to my environmental equipment business. I did this by using the library at the state department of environmental protection. There I found stacks of helpful information. This information can be collected quickly at the right trade shows or professional society meetings as well. Be sure to figure in the cost of attending these events as part of your business investment.

Trade shows and technical conferences
Many times over the years, I have found that visiting trade shows and technical conferences is one of the most efficient ways to gather a variety of information central to starting a new company. Two days of intensive work, going from booth to booth and asking questions, is one of the best ways to

accumulate valuable data. There is a trade show or technical conference for virtually every area of endeavor. They are not hard to get into if you pay the admission fee and check the box somewhere on their form indicating that you are in some way involved with the trade or profession. You can gather product information, industry trends, names and contacts. People who are important in the industry can be contacted and sample issues of trade magazines can be obtained (usually at no cost). You can get access to industry studies, product information, government regulations, foreign trade contacts and much more.

An important plus of attending trade shows is that many of the exhibitors' booths are manned by high-level executives, senior scientists and engineers, key marketing people, and other valuable contacts. Often you can meet the company president pitching his products to passers-by. This may be the one time when you can meet him or her without arranging an appointment weeks in advance or having to pass through a protective phalanx of assistants. Everyone at a trade show is generally on his best behavior, in a good humor, and unusually willing to discuss company, product, and applications information with complete strangers. Use this rare but available opportunity as a new entrepreneur.

*Trade shows are key for market research and promotion. Here
I am at a world ozone congress with a customer from Thailand.*

Deciding which show or conference to attend

The key to getting the most out of the trade show or technical conference is to find the ones focused in the right areas
useful to you. Shows and conferences are advertised promi-
nently in the relevant trade and professional journals. These
journals usually have a special page listing conferences and
shows of interest to their readers. These are listed as "Events"
or "Calendar." One way to find out if a show or conference
is relevant for you is to talk to people in the business in your

target market. See what trade shows they recommend. The next step is to call the organization sponsoring the show to get an information kit. This will include preferred hotel and airline arrangements, entrance forms, and the like. The information kit often includes a listing of technical presentations and a list of exhibitors as well. This data should be an excellent basis for you to decide if this is the show for you to visit. If you are torn between a few shows or you get conflicting recommendations, be prepared to visit two or three. This will be time well spent.

People and Contacts

Anybody who is a success in business will tell you that "who you know" is one of your most important assets in business. When people change jobs, they often say that they took nothing with them except their Rolodex rotary card file which was the most common form of referencing contacts. Now such data is often stored in thumb (flash) drives that are quickly made and easily hidden. The data bank will include potential employees as well as contacts that may never become employees. You cannot always tell ahead of time where and how a given contact might fit into your future. Finding people with the right sets of skills for your available positions and needs is one of the biggest challenges of any business. Your databank may have a potential candidate hidden in it.

When you start your business, you should have a data bank of these contacts listing addresses, phone and fax numbers, and email addresses. When you get phone numbers, try to get extensions or a direct personal number as well as cell phone numbers. Know which department your contact works in. In today's large organizations, it is impossible to find someone through corporate information unless you at least know the department as well as the person's name.

There are many people to consider for your contact list. How about your college professor of chemistry? He could be a crucial advisor or consultant for you now, even though he may have changed jobs and has a new address. What about the old army buddy who could be a great salesman for you after your company is under way? Or the bored bookkeeper you noticed working in the insurance agency?

People you may have thought were interesting but of no value to your proposed business could suddenly be of huge value. Suppose your business changes focus, develops a new product, or has unforeseen problems. Because you cannot predict the future, all of these people should be stored away in your new company's data bank.

People who knew you personally will often put in an extra effort on your behalf when the need arises. Very late in his business career, my grandfather was locked into patent litigation with the U.S. Government. The Army had authorized a Japanese company to manufacture my grandfather's design of a field stove. The Army had not bothered to negotiate a license for the use of my grandfather's patents. When he found out, he was truly David taking on Goliath, particularly in view of the patriotic fervor ablaze during the Korean War, which would favor the Army's case. Luckily, an old college roommate of my grandfather's had gone on to become the Secretary of Commerce. After that, he became a partner in a powerful Washington, DC law firm. My grandfather enlisted his aid when he had to take on the Army. Together they won. You just never know who will come in handy. My advice is do not throw out those old yearbooks or alumni magazines!

Cooperative Development and Strategic Alliances

A recent concept is "cooperative development and strategic alliances." The idea is to create a partnership where there is shared research, shared marketing, or other shared resources. These alliances often spring up between an energetic start-up company and a larger organization. The bigger companies tend to be less venturesome but will have many times more resources than the smaller companies. The partners in such an arrangement are most often two companies, but they can also be between a company and a government agency, a company and a research institute, and others. I have been a director of two high-tech companies where we did shared research with U.S. Government research laboratories. In both cases, the Government laboratory had a patented development which was licensed to the small company. In return, the small business licensee would share with the Government lab new technical insights that it developed. Marketing for these types of alliances often involves shared catalogs, shared databases, cross licensing of brands and various joint promotions.

The cooperative and strategic arrangements work if the organizations involved are not competitive but instead enjoy a symbiotic relationship with each other. These cooperative efforts and strategic alliances never appear on balance sheets as assets, but they are a tremendously valuable resource for many small as well as large companies.

Franchises and Licenses

Franchises

Franchises are essentially licenses to use someone else's know-how and brand name as the core of your independent business. Much of the current new American business dream is getting a McDonald's franchise for a hamburger-hungry growth neighborhood. Or perhaps inheriting a Holiday Inn franchise from Uncle Harry. But there are many other kinds of franchises. These are virtually unknown and often apply to just one product or service that could be offered by your business. For example, you may have a pet store with many products, but to attract the most customers, you might need a grooming franchise.

Franchises are usually awarded to business people who have demonstrated general business ability and who have investment capital. All they need to complete the picture is a business product or service, specialized equipment, furnishings and know-how, and a recognized brand name. The pet store provides complementary products and space which makes the grooming franchiser. Franchises get you going with a recognized brand name or proven process, so they are a great asset to quickly develop momentum for a starting business. Franchises are not free, however, and as long as you own the franchise, you will be paying franchise fees, royalties, and for proprietary supplies.

When you develop the franchise

Do not overlook the possibility of developing a franchise to offer other new businesses. An arrangement like this usually involves rights to manufacture or sell products or services. It will sometimes include the rights to use your trademarks and brand names. For example, if you have developed a new chemical to kill household bugs, you may make more money franchising extermination service businesses who must use your "Bug-Zap" brand of chemical than you would make selling the "Bug-Zap" chemical to various stores. (Imagine a nickel for every bug zapped!) Usually, your business must run on its own for five years or more to develop salable know-how, designs, and a recognized brand name before you can attempt to franchise your package to other businesses.

Licenses

Licenses are legal authorizations to make and sell a product whose design is either proprietary or patented. Licenses are typically granted for a defined territory or application and for a defined period of time. Payments, often called royalties, tend to be based on a percentage of sales. Licenses have been important resources for beginning high-tech businesses. They can help the new business obtain a proprietary product or process to increase sales. Licensing can also move in the other direction. For example, if the new business has a hot invention, it could license someone else to commercialize that invention for cash royalties. There are many pitfalls for the unwary in licensing so I highly recommend carrying out any licensing negotiations with the help of an attorney experienced in these matters.

My grandfather built a multimillion-dollar business out of licensing his patents for oil burners. In the 1930s through the 1950s, they were the predominant oil burner design. While he ran into trouble protecting his patents from unlicensed exploitation, as we have seen with his Army litigation, on the whole, the licensing mode provided him with a more carefree management style than if he had had to do his own manufacturing and marketing. On the other hand, if he had successfully managed a manufacturing and marketing company, he could have made more money. Therefore, the suitability of licensing as a business mode also depends on your personality and how much of your efforts and time you are willing to invest in your business.

For my environmental monitoring equipment business, we did most of our own manufacturing and marketing in part because we did not have any patents by which we could value and enforce a license. We only had specialized know-how. In addition, our market was more limited than the one my grandfather was addressing. Because of the low cost of the product and the limited market base, the total royalties to my company, if licenses were granted, would have been small.

Buildings and Space

Many new entrepreneurs think that their first office, store, or plant should be in an impressive building and location. It is also true that entrepreneurs very often feel that fancy buildings are a suitable monument to themselves once they begin to feel success coming their way. The impressiveness of the building though is neither a reliable guide (nor the path) to the success of the business. Just consider the "No Name," one of Boston's most popular and successful seafood restaurants. It was located in a rundown warehouse on the docks. A wise Boston investor I knew observed about high tech companies: "When they move out of their garrets and into fancy industrial parks, that's the time to sell their stock." He posited that the personnel often lose their frugality and hustle and become more interested in being the lords of the manor. Also, when it appears that the boss is more prosperous, employees become more demanding at salary review time.

In an earlier chapter, I mentioned that I was hired to manage a machinery manufacturing company in Northern New Jersey. When I first saw the plant, I almost took the next plane home. It was a dilapidated pile of bricks that sprawled over a city block. It had started life as a temporary WW II building to manufacture airplane propellers, and 30 years later, it still had not been modernized or torn down. The plant was grimy and full of gaping holes. Wires and plumbing dangled everywhere. Yet the machinists, welders, and other workers were oblivious to all this. They were diligently working the metal of tomorrow's machines. My office, which was small and dark, would be a rare find today. It was completely paneled in heavy walnut, had heavy glass-topped desk, elegant leather chairs, and its own bathroom. This building was an inexpensive space that seemed to stir the creative juices.

The apparent defects of the building were in fact a boon to us. There was no problem doing experimental work on new equipment designs. We could cut through walls, string wires, and lay pipes without fear of damaging anything. We were also in a type of building and a part of town where we did not have to seek municipal approval for our inventive activities.

Then I changed the company over from traditional machinery manufacturing to high-tech instrument development. But what would the high-tech customers think about our quaint but dilapidated old plant? After all, our customers were senior engineers from major chemical companies like Dow and DuPont. They came to observe demonstrations of our equipment working on their materials before they purchased. As the years passed, I learned that our inspiring lab in a run-down building had become legendary. If you were an engineer on the way up, you visited our plant partly because you were on the innovation track, and our crazy facility had a reputation for being a hotbed of innovation.

I later observed an interesting parallel. When I visited the Dows and the DuPonts, I found that the most creative labs were in the older, run-down buildings rather than the new showcase glass palaces where people were afraid to spill a cup of coffee. Creative people often seem to feel less fettered where there are no restrictions on constructing experiments.

Eventually, we had to move out of our old facility because it was being knocked down to make an outlet center. At the behest of our venture capitalists, we moved into a modern plant in an attractive industrial park. The employees became contentious. They certainly did not work any harder. Then the business began a downhill spiral for a myriad of reasons. I still think a major one was that we had moved out of an informal environment, where people enjoyed each other's company and freely shared ideas, into a modern showplace where everyone seemed to become more conscious of their territories, boundaries, and offices. The creative juices just seemed to dry up, and overall productivity declined. The lesson I learned was that a showcase building does not necessarily help the company!

Incubators

"Incubators" are a fairly new concept offered to start-up companies by more and more communities. They are space and service resource centers and are becoming a great incentive for start-up businesses to consider for their first home. Currently, high-tech companies are the preferred tenants. An incubator is a shared space let out for below market rentals. It usually offers shared support services such as shipping and receiving facilities, secretarial services, larger office machines, and even a lounge and lunch area. Because their rents are below comparable local commercial space, long-term leases tend not to be required or encouraged. A company can stay in an incubator only a few years, and then it must let another start-up in. But those few years can be the difference between making it and failing for a new company. You can find out about incubators in your area by calling city, county regional and state economic development departments.

Home as a base
Home basing of a start-up business is also an option. Often the office is in the house and the shop is in the garage or shed. Sometimes entrepreneurs buy a house in the country, where neighbors are distant and there are few or no zoning laws. That way they can build shops, labs, studios, or other special buildings without official hassles. It is nice to have breakfast at home and then stroll across the grounds to your office. Both my father and my grandfather built up multi-million dollar technically based businesses on their expansive properties

Tax laws and zoning restrictions can be detailed and tricky with respect to home-based businesses. For example, small home-based businesses are allowed in my neighborhood, but due to historic preservation regulations, no signs are permitted. To avoid potentially big future troubles, you should check out these laws and restrictions in your area with your local authorities before proceeding.

Machinery and Equipment

Almost every business, whether it is retail, manufacturing, research, or services has at least some specialized machinery and equipment. Any company's specialty machinery and equipment and the know-how on using it effectively, is a very important asset and a key company resource. The equipment can range from big walk-in refrigerators for a restaurant to an assortment of delicate hand tools for a home jewelry business. All your equipment requirements should be determined and costed before you start your business.

Tips on reducing equipment costs
Whatever the equipment it is that you need, when you total the cost of the whole list, you will probably find the price high and beyond what you had first imagined. It is worthwhile therefore to invest a considerable amount of time trying to figure out ways to reduce equipment costs before you begin.

- Look in the classified ads of local newspapers and trade publications for used equipment.
- Buy equipment from established companies in your area who are trading-up to new generation equipment or are shifting their business focus.
- Buy the assets of bankrupt companies at auction. Notices of auctions and the equipment lists are posted in some newspapers and trade publications.

Computers and Software

Nothing has changed the economics of the start-up companies and the administration of small businesses more than computers and software. They revolutionized medium and large businesses in the 50s through the 80s. Now fast PCs and user-friendly application-oriented software are doing the same for small businesses. PCs are currently fast enough and have enough memory capacity to be equal to all general small business requirements. Specialty software for accounting, planning, engineering and Internet browsing is so efficient and easy to use that there is no excuse for not having it in place from the beginning. If you select the right software, you will find you will need fewer staff. You will also have more productivity in all areas, from product design to billing. For a small high-tech company, I have found that an office staff of three in the 70s shrank to two in the 80s and now in the 90s can be done by just one person.

Computers can be purchased new or used. For 10 years I used patched up a used computer. Looking back today, that computer seems like a toy, but like the first car I bought for $50 from a farmer when I was in college, it was a pal. The car, a straight-8 Buick Roadmaster with four holes on each side, was dubbed the Black Moriah. The computer, which still calls up fond memories, could be called the Beige Box.

These days the computer should have the best antivirus software, and nightly off-site automatic backup. It should have current high speed Internet and network interfaces. These will be hard if not impossible to install on an old clunker.

With my first computer and some early DOS programs, I did accounting, letter writing, faxing, customer record keeping, and a few engineering calculations. The point is to get something useable and reliable even if it is not state-of-the-art. Remember, most of the software you acquire now will run on your next computer. Usually, next generation software will absorb this generation of software with no loss of data.

If you really want the latest and fastest equipment, a good justification for it is the time it will save you just on Internet communications.

I have found that having two or more computers is a worth-while expenditure for even a starting business. Backup data can always be swapped from one to the other. If one computer crashes or is stolen, irreplaceable data is not lost. In addition, during business activity peaks one computer may be tied up fulltime on office tasks. The second computer can then be used by engineering, marketing and for other activities without any loss of time or productivity.

Credit Cards

I'll admit it. I financed my first little company by credit card. Almost everyone does to a certain extent. Even mega corporations are doing it when they ask you, the employee, to charge your travel to your *personal* credit card, and they will reimburse you later. They are borrowing on *your* card, and *your* credit line, rather than further borrowing on their corporate card or credit rating.

In the case of my first company, a local bank and American Express teamed up to give every member of my graduating college class a Gold Card. I was scared of it and used it very little. Then I started a home-based management consulting business after working for a few years for a consulting firm. In those days, American Express would never have approved a gold card for an applicant who was a self-employed management consultant! It was a resource that came with me to the business. I used it to pay for food, gas, restaurants, car repairs—almost everything—and I paid the credit card account with the payments from clients, which normally arrived 45-60 days after billing.

After all, you have to start somewhere with whatever advantage you can muster. In time, your success will be noticed, even by your bank. My bank, a little two-branch community bank, noticed my busy little operation after a year or two. Then they refused to take "no" for answer. They insisted on making me a "starter loan." Meantime, the credit card provided the business its liquidity.

Credit cards can be trouble though, and you must avoid becoming a credit card junkie. Calculate the maximum credit card balance you can have and still fully pay the monthly balances. *Never go above that self-imposed borrowing limit.* Credit card companies can force you into bankruptcy if you are hopelessly behind in your payments, although they will generally try to avoid this extreme last resort.

Cash

I will conclude this chapter with more to say about cash. Cash, as they say, is king. It is good for your ego to spend it, but when you run out, that is the ball game. Therefore, a key part of resources management is converting the cash into something else, which will be more valuable to the business than the cash is.

Cash always has to be working for you. It cannot just sit there. You have to be investing now in projects that will take a few years to come to fruition. For example, perhaps some of the cash should be converted to inventory to satisfy those customers who will only buy if you can deliver immediately. Some of the cash should be converted to marketing and product development, because in these areas results may take months or years to realize. Some might go to hiring and training good employees. The key thing is that the investment of the cash be done by experienced people who have a real sense of the dynamics of the business. The directors of the business should see that, in a broad budgeting sense, the cash is being spent prudently and effectively, and that the interest of the investors is being followed.

The most prevalent problem I have seen in high-tech start-ups is when cash turns into an opiate for the entrepreneurs. Frequently, they raise considerably more cash than they need. Then, before the dust settles, it is all gone. Rather than having concentrated on building the business, they fall back to the apparently easier short-term fix of using their new cash to raise more investment capital with the promise of a rosy future just around the corner. For some people it is more fun to produce torrents of cash by pitching investors than to patiently build the business. But with each new investor, the entrepreneur's share of the company declines until one day the awful realization dawns: he has lost control of his own company.

I was a director of a small scientific instrument company that was perpetually running short of cash. Every time a cash problem developed, more cash was raised from investors. I was against this course of action, but my views were in the minority. No staff was cut and often someone was hired. The company grew for a while in this fashion but not because of product sales. I was seriously considering resigning from the board. The tiny company issued 100's of thousands of shares which had finally fallen to almost zero value. At the last moment, a Japanese high-tech conglomerate came along, bought the company for pennies on the dollar, and sent all the directors, including myself, packing. Now the company is focusing, as they should, on making and selling products.

Recognizing and marshaling all your resources and assets that either come with the new business or that you acquire after start-up, is an important key to a successful business. It is in the nature and amount of these resources that your competitive advantage lies.

10

FINANCING YOUR DEAL

Money talks...

I put this chapter near the end of this book for a reason. I wanted to be sure you did all your planning, product development, team building and other essential tasks before going out looking for money. Potential loan officers, investors, and others involved in your venture's finance, will want a minimum of uncertainty and to feel confident that you have done all the spadework first.

Let's say you have your product, your sales projections, and your cost estimates in hand. All you need is the money to start your business. Armed with your business plan and your boundless enthusiasm, you are ready to show potential investors how investing in your "deal" (as investment projects are called) is in everyone's best interest.

You have to be prepared for setbacks, unanswered calls, rejections, and outright rudeness. Looking for capital is on a completely different psychological plane than talking to customers, suppliers, or potential employees. For many people, getting the deal together is the most difficult part of starting a company. The trick is not to take any of the many rejections personally. Do not despair and do not give up!

There are many reasons for rejection at this stage. The person you approach may not be knowledgeable or interested in your market area or business approach. The potential investor may have constraints that you are unaware of, such as policy changes in their organization or in funds supply. Try to build a rapport with every potential investor you approach. It is possible that at some future date, the same investor may be very receptive to helping in your second-round financing, or they may be able to help you in other ways.

Preparing for Your Presentation

It is necessary when looking to raise capital for your new business that you put together a presentation. I have been involved in a great many investment presentations. Many were successful and some were not. To help you prepare for your presentation, I would like to summarize my own observations on success in this area.

Be prepared is key. That means making sure, before you sally forth, that you have thoroughly prepared your business plan and have rehearsed answers to possible questions. Have copies of the plan with you ready to hand out. (Business planning and plans are discussed in chapter four). Nothing will make your case like a solid well-thought-out plan. It will spell out what kind of investment you will need and how it will be spent. It will also show the potential investor how their investment will be paid back.

In order to add detail, credibility and excitement to your presentation, bring along such support materials as product samples, brochures and/or recent advertising, customer testimonials, recent financial statements of your company and pictures of your booth at a recent trade show.

Present yourself like a rising captain of industry. Dress well. This may sound corny, but this is not one of those times to skip wearing a suit.

If you are a good talker and can present your case forcefully, go into the meeting alone. My experience has taught me not to bring along associates or co-presenters because you can lose control of the presentation. The meeting could bog down in trivial points. (Did you ever see a great evangelist with a co-presenter?)

Financial expertise

Unless you come from the financial world, you will not be expected to be an expert in finance. It will be very helpful, however, to have a basic understanding between "debt" and "equity" because the subject is likely to come up repeatedly. Banks are the most common example of *debt holders*. A common form of *debt financing* is automobile financing. The bank does not want your car, they want the interest. Other debt holders are often community development loan organizations, wealthy employees, and even suppliers. Banks cannot make equity investments unless this is done through venture capital or outside affiliates.

Equity financing is different. Perhaps it is best illustrated by the stock market. When you invest in stock in a company, you become a part owner of the company. As such, you want the value of your ownership to grow. *Equity investors* (shareholders) are usually the founding employees, wealthy friends and relatives, individuals called "angels" who invest in local businesses, venture capital firms, and sometimes other companies or entrepreneurs in your industry.

Debt holders, by general commercial law, have "seniority" (priority) over equity holders (shareholders) when the company is in financial trouble. If the company goes bankrupt, the debt holders have first claim to its assets (office equipment, inventory, etc.) when these must be sold. After the debt holders have been repaid from the asset sales, the shareholders divide any leftover proceeds.

Debt financing

Debt financing is financing to the company in the form of loans. When a bank makes the loan, it will be against secured assets. This means that you will be asked to pledge possessions of easily salable value. These can include "receivables" (amounts owing to you from customers), inventory, equipment and real estate. This is all logical enough. A bank, however, will also ask you for your "personal guarantee." This horrifying provision means that in the event of loan default and if your pledged assets do not cover the loan repayment, you will be responsible to make up the difference out of your own pocket. If this means selling your house or adding another mortgage to it, so be it. Frightening as it sounds, this usually is a standard provision for small business loans. You may as well get comfortable with the idea before you start seeking out a loan. Unsecured loans (loans not pledged by assets) are made by individuals, such as your rich uncle, regional development organizations, even occasionally by suppliers. *In times of financial crisis, these types of unsecured loans are often considered to be equity by the power players. If the business were to career towards insolvency, the unsecured loans could rapidly become worthless.*

>>> *I have seen many entrepreneurs try to put their assets out of reach of business creditors by putting the assets in their spouse's name. A word of warning: this is sometimes interpreted as a shell game by the court. If the court sees it as a dodge on your part, the bank will win.*

Equity financing

Equity financing is selling stock in your company. This may seem like a great idea, especially after a bank suggests you might have to give up your house when you get *debt financing*. The problem with selling shares is that you are giving up a piece of your company. When you first start out, this may seem like a small concession, but years down the road that block of stock may prove to be very valuable. You may find yourself wishing you saved it for something else, such as employee incentives. In addition, if there is ever a battle for control of the company, that block of stock could be voted against you, causing you to lose control of your dream. The fact is, nothing is free in business and nothing is without risk. Therefore, go into your venture knowing that each course of action has its pros and cons. It is all a matter of weighing them out.

Using the Web

There are many helpful places to visit on the Web to aid you in your search for financing. I strongly suggest that you take at least a day to familiarize yourself with two Web sites which are inexhaustible sources for small businesses. They cover "where to find and who to contact" information. The basic mother lode for answers to such searches is the U.S. Small Business Administration site at www.sba.gov. There you can find out where in your state you can locate the local SBA office, the office of SCORE and contacts for SBIR grants. It also has information on franchises, women and minorities in small business programs, etc.

Crowdfunding

See "Crowdfunding" in the next section. Crowdfunding is the recent practice of funding a project or venture by contributions from individuals. Project description and promotion is largely through the Internet. A Website which is essentially a commissioned sales agent is involved and is called the "platform."

Finding Investors

Rarely do you get enough financing from any one source. More often, you get some investment here and some funding there. The question becomes: whom are you going to approach about investing in your company? What follows is a list that covers the most common prospects you should consider.

- **Family and friends.** When you first start, there may not be enough company history to satisfy professional investors. But your Uncle Harry has known you for many years and will take a chance with a modest investment. While family and friends may not represent a huge source of investment capital, there may be just enough available to get you going for a year or two. I believe this is a good place to start. There will be fewer formal conditions and commitments involved. If things go well for your company, larger outside investors will be attracted. After a year (or better, three years, if you can last that long on Uncle Harry's money), you can go to institutional investors with charts showing continual progress and other evidence that you're a bankable business person and not just a flash in the pan.

- **Banks.** I have found banks to be an excellent institution to visit early in your search for capital. Even if the bank's own loan programs do not fit your needs when you are first starting out, banks usually know excellent local sources of capital available for small business. They will know, for instance, who to see about U.S. Government Small Business Administration (SBA) loans. They will also know about community development corporation loans. Special programs for women and minorities are often found via the bank loan departments. I have found banks are often underrated as a source of at least some of the financing of small beginning companies. Everyone knows that banks make loans against assets such as a second mortgage ("home equity loan") on your house, but what many people do not realize is that banks can finance the purchases or leases of essential business equipment, such as computers. Some beginning entrepreneurs do not really make an effort to see what's available from banks, believing that nothing is there for an unknown company. Bear in mind that bank loan departments are like anyone else with a commodity to sell: if they have too much capital they often will get aggressive about selling it, and if they do not have enough, they can be very difficult to talk to. If there is aggressive bank management trying to stir up a generally substantial bank, you will often find their loan officers open to discuss relatively venturesome financing. If one bank does not seem receptive to listening to you, try the next one down the street.

- **Angels.** An angel is a new name for an old capital source, namely a wealthy individual who invests in new companies for a variety of motives. We used to call this "Doctors and Lawyers money," because wealthy professionals were often interested in investing in promising local ventures. They could do this without all the paperwork involved with investment institutions. The term "angels" has come into vogue because these local wealthy investors now are more likely to be newly rich entrepreneurs, managers or retired industrialists. Often they will be interested in offering their experience and expertise along with their investments.

  In general, angels are hard to find. They do not advertise in the yellow pages and they do not list themselves on the Web. Angels are most often found through presentations at local investment clubs. They can also be found through the informal network of bankers, lawyers and accountants. In larger cities, there may be angel groups.

  Three generations of my family started businesses with angels—my grandfather in the 1920s, my father in the 1950s and myself in the 1980s. The amounts of money involved were greater than family-and-friends money and less than would interest a venture capitalist. In each case, the angel was someone who knew the entrepreneur. In my grandfather's case, it was his patent attorney. Angels typically invest $10,000-$100,000. This was the experience my family's companies had.

- **Your house.** One way for you to develop a business banking relationship with your bank is to get a home equity loan or second mortgage. Although the loan is to you as an individual, it flows through to the company as your contribution to capital. I recommend getting the home equity loan through your bank, even though many other institutions offer these loans. You should be taking every opportunity of building a relationship with your bank.

- **Credit Cards.** Credit card companies did not have investing in your company in mind when they issued you a credit card, but everybody does it. This is not a source of basic investment capital. It would be considered "working capital" by banks. It is capital used to finance purchases of inventory and services, repaid to you by your customers. I had a one-man management consulting practice for three years that I financed entirely by my American Express card. Credit cards usually max out after $10,000-$25,000, but that may be just enough to cover your office expenses while waiting for customer payments. The card will also give you instant credit with local merchants, such as the office supply store. If you use a credit card, you will not be filling out tedious store credit applications that may be turned down anyway. Credit cards are not a good source for long-term loan capital because their interest rates are very high, but in the short run they can finance you through the ups and downs.

- **Suppliers.** Sometimes a potential supplier of goods (such as inventory) or services (such as a machine shop) will be willing to give you extended terms in order to have your business as one of their customers. This can happen when you infuse them with your vision for an exciting new product and company. They know that you are squeezed for capital. They also know that if they help you now, when you start growing, you may be a very faithful long-term customer. Certainly, your best prospects for this arrangement are larger and older companies which have accumulated capital. Then if you go under, it won't be critical for them.

- **Customers.** A less apparent source of capital is your customers. Twice I have had situations at start-up companies where this happened. We had a product in development that a major customer wanted so urgently that they were willing to pay in advance in order to get expedited delivery. One was a supplier to the automobile industry. He wanted a simple instrument to measure ozone generated by cars. We had an instrument that probably would do the job, after extensive modification. The customer paid up front for the cost of two instruments in order to get a working prototype. I do not think it worked very well in that application, but it was the forerunner of our most successful model of monitoring instrument. In effect, we were receiving product development financing. This kind of opportunity is most likely to arise for high-tech products sought after by large corporations.

- **Leasing.** Why own a piece of machinery if you can lease it? After all, you can lease telephone systems, computers, copying machines, vehicles, machinery, etc. In many cases, no security is required because the items which are leased provide the security themselves. These leases are generally obtained from the manufacturers or distributors of the equipment involved, but they can also be arranged through third parties, such as banks.

- **Employees.** It sometimes happens that employees will work for less than their normal salary in exchange for stock or stock options in the company. Microsoft and many other companies in the computer industry have used stock options to minimize the cash salaries they have to pay and to motivate the employees to further the company goals. In effect, they are financing part of their payroll from future earnings. This is an extremely complex topic, especially when tax regulations are considered, but my short-term advice to start-up entrepreneurs is to be careful. In the very small company, you may be building an unwanted long-term relationship with an employee through their stock-for-pay relationship. I know several companies that paid engineers partially with stock. After the engineers left for greener pastures, they nevertheless continued to hound the companies for inside (confidential) financial information, offers to buy out their stock, and so on. I had a valuable employee leave me to go fulltime on his drug habit. You probably will not want to be tied to your employees after they leave your employment.

- **Incubators.** In order to encourage new small businesses, many communities are starting "incubators." These are buildings with large spaces to rent. They usually feature lower than market rents, some common facilities such as major office equipment and a shipping/receiving area, a common receptionist, etc. Incubator regulations often stipulate that the tenant companies must move out after they have achieved a certain level of success, in order to let other promising new tenants come in. Their denizens often praise incubators because they are a community of small businesses with similar problems to solve. They represent a mutual help network. Because the incubators lower your start-up costs of doing business, they in effect represent partial start-up financing. Often old mill buildings in industrial areas are partitioned into start-up shops and offices for many small businesses. The businesses appreciate the low rents and the atmosphere of mutual assistance. *It is important to remember that when seeking rental space to avoid long-term lease commitments, because if your company runs into financial problems or for any reason should move, the landlord's intransigence can become your biggest financial and legal problem.*

- **Small business agencies.** These include the U.S. Government Small Business Development Administration (SBA) and town, county or state development corporations (often called SBDCs). Bank loan officers will know who these are and can give you introductions. I have rarely seen financing emerge from these institutions, possibly because the paperwork involved can be intimidating. More often, they seem to be valuable for offering volunteer experts to small businesses as "mentors." The best-known source of mentors or advisors is SCORE (retired executives who advise business). They can be found through the Small Business Administration office. Check out all these resources, because you never know where you will hit upon a real nugget of information or a key contact.

- **Government research grants.** The U.S. Government, through its various departments, such as the military and atomic energy commission, publish funding areas for research grants that seem suitable for small business proposals. These are called by various acronyms such as SBIRs, CRADAs, etc. They are almost always focused on new technology development and have as sponsoring organizations the various branches of the Department of Defense, NASA, the EPA and others.

The best place to start your search for these programs and their specific priorities, is through the Small Business Administration's extensive Web site, www.sba.gov. It may take some poking around up and down through various menus, but very detailed information can be found there. I have known a number of small research-oriented companies that have funded much of their operations through these government technology development grants.

- **Regular companies.** Sometimes regular companies that are not in the investment business but who are making products will invest in start-up companies, especially if the start-up represents a window of opportunity. The plastics molding company near you might be very interested in some funding your start-up company if your proposed product will create a market for their plastics products. This would also give them an edge as a supplier. Good candidates are old-line established firms which have accumulated a lot of capital but are looking for fresh ideas and patentable products.

- **Venture capital.** "Venture capital" can come from wealthy individuals, investment partnerships, venture capital corporations, venture capital affiliates of banks, and various other funding sources. Venture capital has become more formal in its requirements over the last few decades. Much of the funding for my enterprises has come from venture capital firms. They tend to look for thorough business plans, a favorable beginning track record and often, but not always, a proprietary high-technology product. They also want to see a team of at least three seasoned executives. They will want about half of the board seats of your company. They generally are not good candidates for financing a start-up company with limited ambitions. They are looking for companies that can "go public" (sell shares to the public) in a few years hopefully as "dot.coms" with explosive growth. When that happens, they can then sell their investment and move on. If you feel that your company is a good candidate for venture capital financing, you should strongly consider retaining an advisor who is experienced in venture capital deals. Venture capitalists generally drive very hard bargains, so before you get too excited about the idea of venture capital, be aware that for every 100 business plans received, venture capitalists may only seriously consider 10. Of that 10 they will fund only one. In general, they like to invest over $500,000 in order to cover the research and administration costs. At this writing, if you have a proposal for a biomedical or Internet venture seeking over $1 million, they will pay rapt attention. If you have a better can opener and are looking for $50,000, you can forget venture capital.

- **Crowdfunding.** The recent practice of funding a project or venture by small contributions from many individuals is called crowdfunding. Project description and promotion is largely through the Internet. A Website, which is essentially a commissioned sales agent, is involved and is called the "platform." This industry, with humble beginnings, often in third world countries, is now booking of $5 billion worldwide. During 2014, 442 crowdfunding campaigns were launched daily. Platforms can easily be found by a Web search.

In the United States, there are three types of crowdfunding:

1 – Rewards. Entrepreneurs promote a product in return for early versions of the product or a keepsake like a T-shirt or coffee mug. This is the most common type of crowd funding. There are few if any regulations and costs.

2 – Equity. The donor receives shares in the company. This is in early stages and is under tight federal Securities and Exchange Commission (SEC) control.

3 – Debt. Popularized by the Lending Club, borrowers are matched with pools of investors.

Crowdfunding has been used for a wide range of ventures including mom-and-pop business, inventions, scientific research, and motion picture projects. Amounts raised typically can range from five thousand dollars to five million dollars.

I have a friend who recently raised eight thousand dollars in crowd funding for his venture to manufacture electric generators powered by ocean wave motion. He gave away coffee mugs and tote bags with the company's logo on them. He thought that effort would appeal to people's sense for supporting environmentally friendly ventures. That did not seem to be the case, and he said the amount of money raised barely covered the costs of raising it. These costs included the platform's commission, the give-away items, and the pay for his employee doing the Internet, shipping, and other tasks involved.

In his opinion, crowdfunding would be much more effective for consumer or small business products. He thought a $99 personal drone would do well.

- **Stock offerings to the public.** This is what everyone dreams about—"going public." But going public generally is not an option for a start-up company and increasingly not an option for those looking for less than about $20 million. Nevertheless, some states are encouraging limited public offerings statewide through special regulations. Regulations vary widely by state. Generally, these regulations come under the heading of "blue sky" laws, where the state wants to protect unqualified investors from risking their savings. Consult with knowledgeable people in your state.

- **Marriage/remarriage.** My grandfather's second wife invested in his company. This source of capital has been used since medieval times or earlier. The flip side of the conjugal approach is that, in my grandfather's case, he lost considerable assets in settling his third wife's divorce.

A business finance scenario

Let's assume you have rounded up a starting financing package. Let's say you got $50,000 from your local bank, secured by a second mortgage on your house. Three local executives who are intrigued by your venture put in another $50,000 each for 25% of the company's stock. You and your spouse put in $50,000 and receive 75% of the stock as the "founders." You are starting out with $250,000 of capitalization, which is a typical amount for a start-up business.

Acting on Behalf of Your Investors

It is time to think about your stewardship of the money put in your trust. You want to keep your investors on your side. They should be rooting for you and not planning your ouster. Here are a few pointers, which will keep the bank and investors feeling positive about you:

- Keep control of the company assets. Only one person should be authorized to sign checks in a small company. That person should be the most senior officer.

- Maintain weekly operating reports on cash, accounts payable, accounts receivable, inventory, taxes due, sales, expenses and operating profits. The latest user-friendly accounting packages for personal computers, such as Quickbooks, make this easy to do.

- Be positive and regular in your reports to the bank and investors. Be seen in the bank's lobby every few weeks so that you can have a casual conversation with the bank officers, and they will recognize you as an up-and-comer worth helping. Give them whatever reports they require, which is usually complete monthly financials. (Bankers actually prefer bad news to no news at all). Send regular progress letter reports to your investors.

- Do not be offended if your investors ask that your accounts be prepared or audited by an independent accounting firm. This is standard practice as companies grow. The challenge for you is to select and direct the accounting firm so that their fees do not overwhelm your fledgling company. Often accounting firms will reduce their rates for you in your first few years with the hopes that they will be kept on as your company grows.

- Be sure you keep accurate minutes at shareholder and board meetings. It is also important to conduct these meetings according to established procedure.

By maintaining a frequent and high level of formal and informal communications with your investors, you will find that almost everyone will be enthusiastic about supporting you with ideas, suggestions, more finance, etc. Enthusiasm can be contagious. Always be ready with a story of yet another company success, such as a major contract just signed. It is much better to talk personally to your bank and investors than to communicate through representatives such as accountants or attorneys. The bank and investors attitude towards your representatives is likely to be, "what are you hiding?"

Other Things to Bear in Mind When Planning for Investments

Start with your own money

A key strategy is to start your new company with as much of your own investment money as possible. If you do, you will not have to give up as much in the early stages. When the company is in its youngest and riskiest stage, investors will want the largest share of the company per dollar invested. They consider themselves "friends doing you a favor." When your company is larger and a proven success, you can sell a smaller portion of your company for a much larger amount of money.

Avoid being pressured by your investors

If you have outside investors to satisfy from the beginning, you may be pressured to do some things too hurriedly. This is the path to crucial mistakes. When I raised a large block of venture capital, my investors thought I should have three vice presidents from prestigious schools immediately. My instincts told me I should not go on this hiring binge, but I felt pressured.

Bringing in that group was probably the biggest mistake I made. It was costly and divisive. By starting small and growing slowly, your new business is less likely to make product development, marketing or personnel mistakes.

Blue sky laws

All states have laws to be sure that you do not sell stock to unsophisticated investors. These are called "blue sky" laws. These laws are to make sure that you accept investors who will not be impoverished if your company goes under. Check with the state governments of your *potential investors*. Find out what forms their state requires. For the most part the blue sky laws are a mere technicality while things are going well. However, if your company should run into severe financial trouble and the investors are unprotected and face total financial loss of their investment in your company, you could be in legal trouble if the relevant blue sky laws were not followed.

Difficulty in buying out early investors

It has been my experience and the experience of other entrepreneurs I have known, that the earliest investors are often the hardest to buy out later. In 10 or 15 years, after you start your company and it has grown to be a success, either you want to buy out the other shareholders so that the company can be passed on effortlessly for estate purposes, or a larger company seeks to buy you out. In either case, it is often one of the first investors who becomes intractable. They may stubbornly resist selling their shares. The rationale seems to be a mixture of emotion and cantankerousness. The attitude is "I was there when you had nothing, and now you're trying to kick me out." This happened to my father when he was simplifying the ownership of his bird feeder company for the purposes of estate planning. He had to buy out his best friend of sixty years, a relationship started when they were eight years old. His friend's investment money had been crucial to starting the business. In the intervening years, my father's business had made his friend a lot of money from that initial investment. Still, the man was crushed after being asked to sell his shares. He sold my father the shares, but he remained very cool afterwards.

Incorporating

If you do sell shares, be sure that your company is incorporated. Even though office supply stores sell do-it-yourself kits for incorporation, I think it is much better to invest in the services of a lawyer who counsels small business. Through their professional advice, you can avoid many pitfalls. As part of your incorporation kit, you usually get a set of by-laws prepared by the lawyer, articles of incorporation, a corporate seal and blank share certificates. I remember when these certificates used to be engraved with eagles, angels or globes and were suitable for framing. Nowadays you get plain printed paper or a magnetic memo. No fun anymore.

When you sell shares, enter them into the registry pages that come with the incorporation kit, usually as part of the certificate book. Recollections can get hazy and controversial a few years hence if all these details are not properly recorded. In the future when you sell shares, you may have to advise and consult with existing shareholders. Typically, they are offered the shares to be sold first as a "Right of first refusal." Be very careful to record all stock transactions and to review any doubtful ones with your attorney.

Be careful passing out Founders' Stock

For many of the same reasons mentioned above, I have found it desirable to avoid the temptation to issue "Founders' Stock" to the first advisors, employees and others who saw you off on the Long March. Everybody's intentions may have been good at the time, but these shareholders may be difficult to buy out later. They may also sell out in the event of a hostile take-over.

I watched a close friend lose control of a large family machinery business. The business was the target of a hostile takeover by a big conglomerate that was scavenging holdings of stock. The non-family stock was publicly traded. The conglomerate got up to 49% of the stock and almost gave up. Then, by a lucky break, they stumbled across an engineer who had over 1% of the shares of my friend's company. These had been given to the engineer early on for reasons no one understood. He had an unsociable personality, made many claims he could not prove and had a reputation clouded by innuendo. That was the takeover company's man! They lit after him like a duck on a june bug. They made him a direct offer for his shares which he sold to them without hesitation. If the family had been more careful in giving up stock over the years, this sad story might never have happened.

Selling stock is not selling product

Never confuse selling stock in your company with selling product. Some entrepreneurs are so visionary and persuasive that they go on selling stock long after they have raised their planned investment capital. When their company is having trouble making enough sales, let alone at a profit, and the company's cash is dwindling, they feel the need to sell more stock based on great success just over the horizon. Meanwhile, the entrepreneur's share of the company is slowly but surely slipping away from him. To avoid this catastrophe, all management and board members should concentrate on making the business succeed with its present resources rather than neglecting the business in the chase for new investment.

Enthusiasm and Financing

If you really believe in yourself, your product and everything that constitutes your company, your chances are good of finding financing. Somewhere along the way you should be able to find someone who has been waiting for your deal. Your enthusiasm, positive attitude and belief in your product will help you through the rough spots as well as kindle excitement in your listeners. Work with your investors as partners and you should be well on your way to success.

You enthusiasm and vision need to be tied to a realistic plan. Be prepared therefore to invest a lot of time exploring financing alternatives and investor candidates. In small business financing there are no pat formulas. Like fishing, you have to just keep at it until you hook the big one.

11

BOUNCING BACK

The life we live is made up of falls and recoveries.
The falls educate us and the recoveries enrich us.

Peter Kilham

I am writing this chapter for the true entrepreneur. If you are one of them, you have had some ups and downs, but you have resolved to learn from your mistakes, find a new vision and path, and start over. Let's say you have gone into business on your own and your venture flopped. I would like to offer you some words of encouragement and help you pick yourself up and get started again. But I should add that you do not have to have experienced failure for this chapter to help you.

Have you ever been on a flight that hit a big air pocket? You sense that you are hopelessly falling and it feels like a bottomless pit. Then, just as suddenly, the free-fall is over. You pinch yourself to affirm that you are alive and that everything is normal again. Then you look out the window and see the sun shining. At that moment life is extra good.

That is what happened with my business, Flow Vision, the company that developed the plastics gel detection equipment described in Chapter one. The instruments we made opened up a whole new frontier in quality control in polymer chemical production. Then, almost overnight, potential customers were canceling purchases of our products. After five years of our sales increasing at a rate of thirty percent or more each year to the polymer chemical industry, there was a major downturn in purchases. A recession had hit and as a result, our customers began cutting back on "discretionary" expenditures.

It was what we came to call "the forklift syndrome." Instead of buying new high tech machinery to improve their product quality, the polymer chemical industry used whatever funds were available to buy another forklift for the warehouse. It was the "safe" way for our potential and previous customers to spend their departmental budgets. They knew the forklift would be unquestioned for its usefulness. Justifying our polymer gel-detecting instrument, whose need and performance could be questioned, could be a one-way ticket to the unemployment line!

As our sales dropped and cash balance plummeted, our investors became nervous. They saw the "waterfall" coming. They feared we would start consuming more of their investment dollars in a futile attempt to keep our sales at a profitable level. One day we would pitch over the edge like a canoe at Niagara Falls, and then rescue attempts would be futile. When I suggested cutting staff so that we could continue to meet payroll, the investors decided my vision had faltered. They were anticipating a bolder, more visionary plan to rebuild the company and since I had none, they lost faith in me.

>>> *In the eyes of investors, the most logical solution to a problem can seem like the wrong one. They expect a vision from the entrepreneur and leader. Doubt and distrust often develop when*

that vision seems to falter. Once that happens, the entrepreneur and the investors are no longer willing dance partners.

My venture capital investors stopped returning my phone calls, yet every few days they issued ultimatums either to produce a miracle or let them sell the company's assets as salvage. They appointed a "yes man" to manage the daily affairs of the company, while I was named chairman and told to stay out of the way.

My most immediate problem was the bank. I knew as soon as the bank sensed the company's problem, they would call in the loan. Then the financial burden would fall on me personally. When banks loan money to new ventures, the founder (in this case *me*) is expected to guarantee the loan with his/or her personal assets. It does not matter that the professional venture investors put in much more money and would have more back-up resources. The entrepreneur and founder is supposed to commit so much personal assets that he or she cannot back out. I believe the thinking of venture capitalists is that your panic will energize you into saving their investment.

In the worst case, if the company is going under—and that could happen because the big investors withdraw their support—then the founder/entrepreneur/leader faces losing everything including his or her house. When I sensed this possibility on the horizon, I quickly made my condominium a joint property with my wife. The bank could still seize it, but even hardened bankers will try almost everything to avoid kicking a family out of their house.

There was one venture capital investor, Richard Dumler from Drexel Burnham, who still seemed sympathetic to my plight. The others seemed happy to forget about this venture and move on to other more promising ones. He said he would go to the bank with me and help me plead my case or at least provide moral support. We went to an ice cream parlor, of all places, across the street from the bank. We had chocolate ice cream sodas and reviewed possible scenarios and responses, as a lawyer might do with his client before a trial.

Then we went to see the bank officer who was in charge of disposing of our case. He was called the "workout man" although "executioner" seemed more to the point. The elevator went up what seemed like endless floors. We walked past acres of secretaries. The workout man was sitting at a small desk in the middle of a large dark room. His desk had folders of documents detailing bank investments that had gone bad: trailer parks, office buildings, auto body shops, you name it. He motioned us over to two dilapidated chairs. Clearly, this was not the New Customer office.

The workout man looked at us for what seemed like an eternity. I tried to look composed, but inside I was fidgeting and sweating. He looked weary and almost too tired to say anything. Then he said, "I dunno. Probably it's our fault. We shouldn't have loaned you that much." Richard gave me a thumbs up sign indicating that the bank would not call in their loan. The free fall of me into a financial black hole seemed to have been arrested. Still, I could not wait to get out of there.

Richard sensed that the workout man wanted *something* in return though. He also knew that we would probably be sold to a larger company for only a little better than liquidation value. He mentioned this to the workout man and offered the bank royalties on the sales our company would make after it was purchased. Although hardly salvation for the bank's loan, the workout man readily agreed because it was at least a face-saving proposal.

What Richard had done was to save my personal assets. They were secure because the bank would not call in the loan I had guaranteed. That was good, but I was now without a remunerative occupation. I knew my next few months would be occupied by the non-paying job of inventorying the company's assets, laying off employees, making arrangements with creditors, talking to investors and countless other unpleasant tasks. I felt like my whole life up to that time had been wasted. My only reliable friend seemed to be my wife, Betsy.

Then a prosperous small company, specializing in mostly military airport radar systems, decided to make us an offer. Our company represented a promising avenue for commercial diversification for them. My dreams came alive again. The faithful at my company thought that it was only a matter of time before our chemical and plastics customers would resume buying again. It was hoped that versions of our technology could be used in other industries such as papermaking. Things began to look a little better.

In a maneuver called "cram down," the company's creditors were asked to accept twenty cents on the dollar (alternately, they might receive nothing) for what the company owed them. They pretty much had to agree. But cajoling was required to get a sufficient number of the creditors to agree to our offer. I can report that it was a lot less fun than inventing the product. I would spend hours reading threatening letters from bill collectors, writing proposals to our creditors, and calling the creditors to see if they would agree to our greatly reduced payment terms.

The company which was rescuing us basically purchased all our assets for next to nothing. They offered some cash, royalties and stock to our preferred stock shareholders, who were the venture capital investors. The early development team and

I were to receive virtually nothing for our stock. I was offered a three-year consulting contract, which is not an uncommon practice in these situations.

The buyer wants the creative visionary on board, but not in a position of direct management. The buyer also does not want the visionary working for a competitor. In addition to the consulting contract, I was offered a stock option. I knew this was worthless at the time of the offer, but I accepted it anyway. Years later, when the company that acquired my company was itself acquired, my stock option suddenly had significant value.

I was picking myself up and accepting anything. Several companies in the chemical instrumentation industry gave me very remunerative consulting projects. For many people, the story might have ended here.

Not for me though. A new thought began to gnaw at me. Several major customers of Flow Vision, my old plastics gel detection instrumentation company, had said that the future was in environmental instrumentation. Over and over, I was told that these companies were spending more on environmental instrumentation than on process instrumentation. The CEO of DuPont, who I met by chance in a DuPont cafeteria, said CEO really stood for "Chief Environmental Officer." All this was inexorably drawing me to a new business challenge.

There were many expensive and sophisticated environmental monitoring instruments being sold to industry at that time. There was very little however, in the way of simple, low cost instruments which were virtually disposable and which untrained personnel could operate. My new idea called for some creative electronic engineering, which I love doing. Sketches and electronics began to spread around the kitchen table. It was all very therapeutic for my wounded ego. This venture seemed the right thing to do at this time. In 1991, I started my new company, Eco Sensors, Inc.

I was the unpaid chief engineer, salesman, shipping clerk and everything else. The first instruments were for monitoring hydrocarbon gases called VOCs (volatile organic compounds). I stumbled into an immediate niche market. Hospitals needed the application to detect highly toxic and explosive leaks of sterilization gas. The market was not huge but enough to jump-start my little company and helped to restore my confidence in myself.

Even though I had gained many business insights from the ill-fated Flow Vision venture, I knew capital would be difficult to raise because of its demise. Fortunately, our household had the income from my consulting along with my wife's salary. We had no children to support and my wonderful wife said she never wavered in her confidence in me. I was filled with hope for my new company.

About a year later, my father, who was still running his flour-ishing bird feeder business into his 80s, passed away along with my wife's mother. Both had lived in the northeast. Our East Coast ties and commitments were dwindling. We decided to take the start-up business and move west to my birthplace in Santa Fe, New Mexico. An additional pull for me was remem-bering my mother's father, James L. Breese, Jr., who had built his very successful oil burner business in Santa Fe. Although he was long gone, I was sure that he would help. In some curi-ous way he did because my little environmental business has flourished and grown in our charming Spanish colonial town. We had no debt, we were the world leaders in our niche, and I had some wonderful employees working with me.

In 2007, I received an offer I could not refuse from a larger gas instrument company in the San Francisco Bay area. This was a result of talking to prospective buyers at a trade show in Los Angeles. I actually received three fairly good offers. Unforeseen to me at the time, the 2008-2013 recession (some would say "crash") in the following years would have made a satisfactory sale at a good price virtually impossible. I am on their board. My company, Flow Vision, now a division of KWJ Engineering, continues to grow and be profitable. We enjoy visiting the Bay Area.

What this whole experience means is that you have to work your way out of bad situations as best you can, regroup, and then see what you can do to revitalize your dreams. You cannot let your fear of failure overcome your desire for success. Fate deals all of us some bad hands. Your job is to not let these be the end of the game. What you have to do is to access your real strengths and build on them the next time around. I advise taking some personal inventory. Look back and ask yourself:

- What are my strengths? Technical? Sales? Administrative? Finance?
- What are my general positive qualities: A sense of humor? Tenacious research? A way with people? Innate optimism? A strong sense of responsibility?
- What business area do I know most about? Computers? Environmental science? Animal husbandry? Home economics? Stock market? Retail?
- What are my dreams really saying to me?

After Flow Vision went under, I decided I was too old to go back and work in somebody else's bureaucracy. But I was also old enough to have learned a few tricks about small high-tech business. I stumbled into environmental monitoring instruments, but if I had not found that opportunity, something else in the instrumentation business would have come along. I just knew that life would wind up presenting me with a satisfying and successful high-tech business.

My father reflected on these matters in an interview with a local newspaper:

My ideas aren't guaranteed to make anyone's fortune. But then again—if you're not in a hurry—maybe they will. You ask me how I came up with a bird feeder that made the world beat a path to my door? By doing my work according to these notions:

1. ***Make sure you satisfy yourself.*** *Don't let yourself be rushed into doing things you're not proud of.*
2. ***Don't be afraid to fail.*** *Be willing to work by trial and error. That's the only way you learn.*
3. ***Reach for excellence always.*** *You can never reach that perfection yourself, but if you try as hard as you can that's the main thing. That's where happiness lies. And, often, success as well.*

ABOUT THE AUTHOR

Larry Kilham is from the third generation of a family which has produced notable inventors who built successful businesses. The author, a Sloan School of Management graduate from MIT, has three patents and has founded two high-tech companies. In 1986 Larry was the co-recipient of the IR-100 Award cited by *Research & Development* magazine for developing one of the 100 most significant technical products of the year. His experiences range from complex defense systems analysis to tiny device development.

Larry lives in Santa Fe, New Mexico and is keenly interested in AI, ecology, global resources and the science of complexity. More information about his books and his blog can be found at www.FutureBooks.info. He can be contacted at lkilham@gmail.com.